في ذكرى

مارك لينز

Off Limits

New Writings on Fear and Sin

Nawal El Saadawi

Translated by Nariman Youssef

GINGKO

First English edition published in 2019 by
Gingko
4 Molasses Row
London sw11 3ux

First published in the Arabic by Masr El Arabia in 2018.

This first paperback edition published in 2020.

ISBN 978-1-909942-47-9
e-ISBN 978-1-909942-44-8

Typeset in Minion Pro by MacGuru Ltd
Printed in the United Kingdom

www.gingko.org.uk
@GingkoLibrary

Content

Publisher's Note

She has been called the Simone de Beauvoir of the Arab World: Nawal El Saadawi – public health physician, psychiatrist, author and advocate of women's rights.

Born in Kafr Tahlah, Egypt, on 27 October 1931, Dr Saadawi has fought all her life for women to be accorded rights over their own bodies. She has campaigned against the brutal harm caused by FGM, fought for a woman's right to pass on her name to her child, and has tirelessly stood up for women's rights in divorce, property and inheritance cases. For her beliefs and endeavours Nawal El Saadawi has endured imprisonment and exile. Her publications have brought her acclaim and criticism in equal measure. She stood as a presidential candidate at an age when others might consider retirement. 'At a time when nobody was talking,' Margaret Atwood said when interviewed for *BBC Imagine*, '[El Saadawi] spoke the unspeakable.'

Dr Saadawi has never shied away from controversy. In 1968, she founded *Health* magazine and a year later published *Al-mar'ah wa al-jins* (*Women and Sex*), for which she was expelled from her position at the Ministry of Health. In 1981, she was imprisoned for her involvement with the feminist magazine *Confrontation*. In 1982, El Saadawi founded the Arab Women's Solidarity Association (AWSA) and later served as editor of the organisation's publication, *Nun*. The Egyptian government closed down the magazine and the organisation barely ten years after its foundation. Undeterred, El Saadawi continued her work, publishing and protesting, facing legal challenges from political and religious opponents and, eventually, exile. In 2002, a fundamentalist lawyer tried to forcibly divorce her from her husband. In May 2008 she won a case brought against her by Al-Azhar University that included charges of apostasy and heresy.

By publishing *Off Limits*, Gingko presents the reader with an original voice, raw and unfiltered, and a powerful representation of feminism in the Middle East. This is Nawal El Saawadi's in her own words: translated, but not adapted or expurgated to comfort a Western audience; not smoothed over to avoid sensitivities; not explained nor excused in order not to ruffle feathers.

'A WOMAN'S VOICE IS REVOLUTION!' Dr Saadawi writes in this book. Listen to her voice and you will find that it will move and unsettle you, but never fail to challenge.

Gravity and the Forbidden Apple

When I was a child, I used to gaze at the sky – like perhaps all children do – and ask my mum and dad: 'Where do the moon and the sun and the stars come from?' I assumed the earth was flat and immobile, then I learned it was shaped like a ball, spinning in space. And I wondered why was it that, if the earth was spinning, I didn't feel it move at all.

When I got a bit older, other questions started to occupy my mind: 'Why does the earth orbit the sun and not the other way around? How does the moon stay suspended in space while orbiting the earth and is not pulled towards the earth by gravity?' Most answers I received did more to obscure than to illuminate: 'It's just how things are;' 'This is how God made the world;' and 'It's nature's way.'

But Isaac Newton has formulated the law of universal gravitation, with which his name is forever linked, as follows: Every object attracts every other object in the universe with a force directly proportional to the product of their masses and inversely proportional to the square of the distance between their centres. That is, the higher the masses of two bodies, the stronger their attraction towards one another, and the higher the distance between them, the weaker the attraction. So that, given the same distance, the attraction between two elephants is stronger than the attraction between two rats.

Any living body or physical mass has the potential to attract – the earth, the sun, the moon, the stars and all the planets.

So does gravity occur among animate physical bodies alone? Is there no attraction between inert objects?

A piece of rock for instance? A piece of rock isn't dead; it is part of the earth, and the earth is a living planet that pivots on its axis and orbits the sun.

And what about attraction between people? Friendship, love or hatred? Why does a person become attracted to another person specifically among all the others? Could it be because of the gravity between two souls?

Humans struggle against the forces that surround them and which pull them towards this way and that. Among these forces are the gravity of the earth and the pressure of the air, their own body mass or weight. A human being is just another mass like all the rival living bodies floating across the boundless universe.

Why doesn't the moon fall to the earth like an apple from a tree? Because the force of the sun's gravity is greater than that of the earth, which keeps the moon moving in the sun's orbit as well, living in suspension between the sun and the earth, like the other planets and satellites that orbit the sun. Newton once said that we live on the earth adrift in the boundless universe.

Is it just the earth that is adrift in the boundless universe? Isn't the moon also lost between the different forces that attract it? As are the sun and the stars and all the planets turning on their axis and orbiting the more powerful planets?

And when it comes to humankind, do not the weaker move in the orbit of the stronger? Could the same not be said of countries too, with the smaller states orbiting the bigger and the more powerful?

What does power mean in this context? Military power? Money, authority, physical strength?

Some scholars imagine that life (or the soul) can live beyond the death of the body and continue to have its own force or gravity. Newton believed in the existence of a soul independent of the body. He further believed that the new laws of physics were proof of the existence and omnipotence of God. Newton, like some other eighteenth-century scientists, had religious beliefs.

In the twenty-first century, most scientists have returned to Democritus's old theory which considers matter as the origin of the universe. Everything is composed of atoms that are constantly diverging and converging. The philosophical debate rages to this day.

Other – non-human – beings are not so preoccupied by what we call the soul. It is a primarily human invention.

In the holy books, the story of the forbidden apple that Adam was tempted by Eve to eat symbolises sin caused by the attraction between a male body and a female body, an extension of the attraction between earth and heaven, between good and evil.

When Newton entered into a conflict with the German

scientist Gottfried Wilhelm von Leibniz over the intellectual property of differentiation and integration (calculus) in mathematics, each maintaining that he was the inventor of the equal sign, the issue was brought before the Royal Society in Britain. The Society ruled in favour of Newton, who happened to be its president at the time! And so, Newton became the inventor of calculus. It also turned out that the story of 'Newton's apple' had originated nowhere but in the imagination of its protagonist, who possibly wanted to establish a link with the tree of knowledge in eternal paradise.

The Most Pious Men in the World

Two historically linked battles rage in the world today on the subjects of gender and racial equality.

The first battle can be observed in Tunisia, the most progressive amongst Arab and Islamic countries when it comes to women's liberation. Since the rise of the women's movement during Bourguiba's rule, there has been the prohibition of polygyny by law, as well as the restriction of divorce to the courtroom and by the consent of both husband and wife. Under Tunisia's former president, the late Caid Essebsi, equality in inheritance and in marrying non-Muslims was established. All that is left to do now is to establish equality in parentage and allow for the mother's name to be honoured alongside the father's.

The frontiers of the second battle are in the United States, which was one of the first countries to officially abolish slavery at the time of Abraham Lincoln. But slavery persisted under different guises, embellished by effusive words surrounding democracy, free elections, neoliberalism, religious freedom and the free market.

In Tunisia, the vast majority of government and public institutions were in favour of gender equality. Only a handful of religious scholars objected when either Bourguiba or Essebsi were in power, only the kind who believe that 'Eve's sin' is carved alongside the sin of knowledge in the *lawh mahfouz* (*tablette préservée*), inerasable by the passage of time; the kind who believe in fixed definitive texts that are closed to (re)interpretation and change. The God they believe in created women from men's crooked ribs, made them men's property, bound them to submission and obedience, and gave their husbands the right to discipline them with just the permissible amount of beating, to divorce them with just a word, and to marry others as they please. A man may even be excused for killing his wife if she seeks her freedom, just as a master could kill his slave, or a ruler kills or imprisons rebels.

But Bourguiba and Essebsi did not cower before the politicised forces of religion. They ignored accusations of apostasy or threats of burning, freed Tunisia of the followers of the fixed text, and led the way for other Arab and Muslim countries towards freedom and dignity. For there can be no freedom or dignity for anyone in a country where half the population is subjected to systemic humiliation. Tunisian men used to be able to divorce their wives as easily as they took off their shoes. Just one word – *taleq* (you are divorced) – and the wife would find herself out on the street. As is still the case for us in Egypt today, in spite of our deep-rooted civilisation which gave us the Ancient Egyptian goddess Maat, a trailblazer of universal justice, and Isis, the goddess of knowledge and wisdom.

Today we have women whose minds are veiled even if their hair, arms, legs and knees are exposed. Some of these women are members of supreme councils, directors of large organisations, university professors and lecturers. Yet they believe their husbands have the right to wed four wives in order to satisfy their sexual urges throughout the month, as – you guessed it – these accomplished women would never dream of allowing themselves sex during menstruation.

Nothing has been found in zoology to say that bulls or donkeys exercise this kind of unchecked, unbalanced sexual gluttony. All the while our family law grants a human husband the right to send his wife back to her family if an illness or disability makes her unable to serve him and/or satisfy his sexual needs.

Where is the collective voice of Egyptian women in the political arena? Successive governments have succeeded in crushing all popular liberation movements, including the women's movement, and encouraged the rise of fundamentalist religious political groups to snuff out any glimmer of free thought. Women's rights were reduced to just opposing the veil, following in the footsteps of Huda Shaarawi's defining moment in the first half of the last century. But women's hijab is only the tip of the iceberg. The main problem remains the darkness that veils the mind, the absence of free and creative thinking, in the sciences and arts as in politics, economics, culture, history, philosophy, religion and ethics.

Our intellects have become incapable of detecting duplicity in the values and laws we blindly follow. We are unable to expose the domestic and external political and economic forces hiding behind the guise of religion, which have ransacked our resources and our minds. Now the Egyptian society easily considers a woman's – or a young girl's – exposed head to be an obscenity. At the same time, a young girl can as easily be married off to a ninety-year-old man. We have lost the ability to criticise contradictions. Beauty products are still marketed to hijabi women – they shape their eyebrows and colour their lips, using all sorts of cosmetics, and get face-lifts, all in the name of modern femininity. Wherever we look, we see cheap entertainment posing as art, hackneyed cinema, mediocre media, and advertisement crowded with naked bodies. Political religious factions have thrived on corruption, accustomed as they are to hypocrisy and deceit. They claim that equality between women and men is an indecent Western tradition that threatens our morality, destroys the God-made feminine vulnerability that men find attractive. And well, what if a man is entitled to inherit twice a woman's share? That's only because it is his responsibility to support her. They make those claims in the face of actual statistical evidence that more women than men are financially responsible for their families.

Another commonly held belief is that marrying a non-Muslim defiles a Muslim woman and sullies her purity, as if among the billions of humans on the earth only Muslim men are pious.

How Far from My Parents Have We Come?

Could anyone – man or woman – be free while living in dependency on another? Could a country be independent while surviving on external aid? The same question haunts me whenever the issue of gender inequality is discussed, and whenever the sore point of American aid surfaces, since Sadat became president in Egypt.

I remember what my father used to say, back when I was a child: 'Free men and women only eat what they have worked for.' He was critical of traditional sayings like: 'A free woman will starve but not eat with her breasts' – a contradictory, treacherous phrase in itself which treats women like mammals and not human beings. To this day, the rights of women are still not fully represented in human rights declarations.

My father was born during the first year of the twentieth century. He excelled in his studies at Al-Azhar, Dar al-Ulum, the Islamic Judiciary School and the Teachers College. He was nominated for a scholarship in a French university when a less competent colleague with better connections took his place. That colleague returned from Paris to become an illustrious minister and acclaimed intellectual. My father could have gone down in history as a famous man, if he had shown more obedience to the powers that be. But as it were, he lived marginalised and forgotten, opposed to the monarchy and to British control, and critical of the ministry of education curricula and the teachings of religious institutions. The Azhar Supreme Sheikh, meanwhile, praised the good king and issued prayers for his long life. My father was relegated to the role of a judge, only to be confronted in the courtroom by the same advocates of the definitive and unchanged authority of the text, the same deniers of *ijtihad* and *tajdid*, whose voices are particularly loud when it comes to women.

My father had come of age in the countryside. He had seen women work the fields, seen them grow produce and put food on the table, supporting their families alongside their men, or – more often than not – on their own, when husbands died of bilharzia, or orally divorced them – by simply uttering the word *taleq* while expelling a post-dinner burp – or took another wife on a whim, or a third or a fourth, or denied their own children to spite their mother or to spite their family. There were so many trials and tribulations that left a woman as sole provider for her family, or cut-off from her support system, but statistics ignored the labour of female farmers and housewives, and other forms of unpaid servitude imposed on women, ignoring women's significance as a pillar of capitalist economy. Since the dawn of patriarchy, legislations have ignored the rights of women, be it in family law, criminal or civil law; that is because women have lacked an organised political power. There was no women's union to campaign and protest, like labour unions or anti-slavery unions back in the day.

Promoters of the authority of an unchanged and definitive text ignore the tragedies caused by issues of inheritance, parentage, oral divorce and polygamy. They ignore the destruction of family values that ensues and the subsequent overpopulation which everyone acknowledges as a problem.

Eighty-five years ago, my father stood in a sharia court (before those were abolished) and defended the inheritance of a woman whose husband had orally divorced her after she had spent her whole youth working the land alongside him. How could the law deny her a share in the land she worked on just because the husband uttered a certain word before he died? My father also defended a woman's right to divorce by *khul'* (divorce initiated by the wife). More than half a century before a *khul'* law was actually passed he argued in court that it was a right granted to women by the sharia itself.

At some point in my youth, I agreed to marry a wonderful non-Muslim man, who was willing to convert to Islam. But my father told him, 'What matters is a person's essence, and I trust my daughter and believe in her right to choose. Besides, adopting a faith just for the purpose of marriage is as meaningless as (unquestioningly) inheriting a faith.' That man was a fellow medical doctor who worked at the hospital for respiratory diseases. He caught tuberculosis from one of the patients under his care and died before we had a chance to live together. That faraway day is documented in my book *My Papers, My Life* which was published twenty-four years ago. It came back to me yesterday as I followed the impressive victory for women in Tunisia: a legislation on the equality between genders, based on the Tunisian constitution which considers a woman's right to choose a partner – regardless of religion, nationality or gender – at the heart of her personal and moral freedom. I thought of my father, who died sixty years ago, and remembered how he and my mother encouraged me to be honest and taught me to focus on the core truth of a person, and to ignore appearances and inherited discrimination.

A Sweet Murderous Woman

'It's easier for me to wield a metal cutter or a welding torch than to make a cup of tea,' said Ahlam Tarek Ibrahim, an Egyptian woman from Hurghada, Red Sea governorate. Her words are subversive. Cutting metal is a man's work, while a woman is supposed to make tea.

Division of labour by gender is not a law sent from heaven or dictated by eternal and unchanging nature. It changes all the time. But it seems that even modern psychology is incapable of keeping up with the speed of change in human nature, and would sometimes go as far as to consider a woman such as the one mentioned above too masculine, depriving her of her uniqueness and creative human character. For how could a medical professional understand a creative and intelligent woman with Freud's theories and the sacred patriarchal teachings tainting his view? The majority of male medics, writers, thinkers – in Egypt and around the world – see 'woman' as a mystery, as if she comes from a different species, one without intellectual ambition or human dignity, her ultimate happiness lying in marrying one of their kind and bringing him tea while he reclines on the bed with a book or sits behind his desk thinking and writing. I have known the wives of major intellectuals, in Egypt and elsewhere, who have no ambition outside their homes, no independent agency that is not tied to their husbands; a wife like that derives her happiness from her husband's self-fulfilment, and buries deep within herself her grief over her own wasted subjectivity, which could eventually drive her to depression or illness or – if it weren't for fear of God – suicide. I have known creative women artists and writers and intellectuals, Egyptians and otherwise, who lived alone and partnerless simply to be able to continue their creative work.

Most psychology experts don't understand women's subjectivity independently of her husband and family. They miss the point when they don't see that the biggest regret in a woman's life is failing in her own self-fulfilment, not failing in love, marriage or motherhood. Why would a woman prefer cutting metal to making a cup of tea? Could it be because she inherited the powerful genes of the goddess Isis, or from a farmer grandmother who dug into earth with a hoe, or a labourer mother who climbed scaffolding while bearing bricks and stone on her back? What matters most in any case is childhood training. As a child, Ahlam Ibrahim worked with her father in his ironsmith workshop. Her father had enough awareness and courage to break out of inherited traditions and train his daughter to cut metal with fire and to face life's difficulties with a strength that exceeds that of men. Maybe he didn't have a son, or maybe he couldn't train his son to do the same. It is good luck for a girl sometimes to have a lazy or incompetent brother so that her father has no choice but to rely on her. Maybe the daughter simply liked ironwork and excelled in it, to the point that cutting metal has become easier for her than making a cup of tea. Such a sentiment could only be expressed by someone who has tasted self-respect and the sweetness of creative work, experienced the pleasure of freedom and independence, and the happiness of self-fulfilment – that is, the fountains of true happiness for anyone, man or woman. The words of the simple iron worker were spontaneous but revelatory of a genius subjectivity that has tasted the joy of being freed from millennia-old traditions. She reminded me of a weightlifting champion who once said that she found weights lighter than housework.

Housework is considered the work of women, along with obedience and submission to the man's absolute authority. This is the root of the humiliation and frustration that women go through. I've hated the kitchen and domestic chores since my childhood. Any man who tried to push me into that sort of labour, even if he was a national hero, got nothing but excision from my life. At the start of my medical career I worked in heart surgery, performing lobectomy on tuberculosis patients. Cutting a chest open with a scalpel was easier for me than peeling a single onion in the kitchen!

Lauded traits of femininity are meant to include peeling onions and scrubbing toilets, while also breadwinning alongside the man of the house, all done thanklessly. But what about the Palestinian freedom fighter who favours the liberation army over a quiet life with her family? How is it that she is able to choose to carry a machine gun over making tea for her husband? How is it that she can use the veil to hide a weapon but not her face? And how is it that fighting, in the case of war, becomes a heroic act and not a sign of crude masculinity that negates her feminine nature?

When I was in prison, I met a woman who had murdered her husband when she caught him in her bed with another woman. She was very sweet and soft-spoken. No one could believe she could be capable of murder. I heard her say, 'I couldn't hurt a fly, but I could kill a man who betrayed my trust.'

My Life's Companion

I'm woken from a deep sleep by the phone ringing. With eyes still closed, my hand reaches for the handset and brings it to my ear. No one would dare wake me up at this hour except her.

'What time is it?'

'The sun set a while ago…'

'Yeah?'

'Yep.'

'Where did it go?'

'To the other hemisphere.'

'And where am I?'

'In Egypt.'

The word 'Egypt' rings in my skull, drilling through the flesh and bone to reach the brittle, amorphous substance within the body, perhaps non-existent outside the imagination, called the soul.

My plane landed in Cairo Airport at midnight the night before, back from a land covered by snow, clad in a fur-lined leather coat, an ears-reaching woolly hat and a big scarf wrapped around my neck and head, from sub-zero cold to the over 40 degrees heat that rose from the ground and bore through my thick boots into the soles of my feet.

I slept for three whole days before I was rid of what they call jet lag.

We agree to meet at the swimming pool at 7am, as we've been doing since we were kids. She loves to swim and only comes alive on the beach, while I adore walking the streets of the city and can only live right at its heart.

It's April, the start of Spring, and the lido in the southern district of Cairo sparkles under a soft sun that takes me back to the days of my youth. For a moment I forget myself and set off running, until I'm stopped by the painful truth: my knees are not young anymore and they don't like to run.

She beats me to the swimming pool like she always does. She's wearing that blue swimsuit with white stripes and swims like a fish born in the sea. I was born on dry land. I always overtake her when walking while she's always ahead underwater.

'New love?'

'You think of nothing but love?'

'Is anything more important?'

'Sure.'

'Like what?'

Two days ago, two churches in Tanta and Alexandria were blown up by Islamist terrorists and Syria was bombed by American terrorists using Tomahawk rockets.

'Toma-what?'

'Hawk.'

She laughs. She has a distinct laughter that works like an anti-depressant, so I laugh with her. Though not exactly like her, because however much I laugh, my laughter remains sane and balanced, within the limits of reason.

She, on the other hand, knows no limits. She lives everything fully, joy and grief, always ready to drive every experience to its climax. She doesn't know middle grounds or
moderation, and would die laughing or crying. Seeing my
laugh, she pushes out her lower lip in mock contempt.

'You're so self-possessed!'

'And you're crazy.'

'While you were away, I met someone…'

'Oh, do I really want to hear this?'

My Cousin Naima's Son

I remembered his mother Naima when I came across the story of his comrade in arms, Abdelhamid Taha Abdelhamid. They have both been buried in Sinai's sands since the war of June 1967, missing with hundreds or thousands of other young men that were buried in the sand and disappeared, entering the records under 'Missing in Action'. Naima's tears back then could have filled the Nile. She would say, 'If only I could see him dead, the burning in my heart wouldn't be so unbearable.'

Damn all those who don't know a mother's grief and consider women half-human.

The remains of his colleague Abdelhamid were found yesterday, 11 April 2017, during the construction of a new road in Sinai. He had his ID, stating his hometown as Tawfiqiya in Fayoum, along with a picture of the girl he was engaged to in December 1966, more than half a century ago.

No Virtue Without Freedom

If you are locked in a room and forced to be virtuous, you get no credit for your virtue.

There's only one way to measure a person's virtue, and it does not change based on gender, class, religion or any other form of identification.

Virtue entails the freedom to act virtuously.

Freedom is a necessary condition for morality.

Morality cannot be imposed through punishment and reward. It is a way of life that starts in early childhood. A girl or a boy learns early on, for instance, the gratification and contentment that honesty brings, and learns also that lying brings with it suffering and lack of self-respect.

The most important lesson I learned from my parents in early childhood was to respect my own mind, and to trust myself, my character and my morals, which empowered me to resist the incessant attempts of school teachers to reject my intellect and mock my independent manner of thinking.

What makes human intelligence special is its ability to grow, adjust, and change everything including itself. With the mind's development, a man's or a woman's character develops too; their understanding of concepts of femininity, masculinity, and morality and honour gains an intellectual character to reflect integrity, honesty, justice, freedom, beauty, creativity – instead of being fixated on things like head-covers, rituals and circumcision. We end up with men and women of high moral standards, capable of resisting any obstacles and forces meant to cage their minds within fixed roles imposed by the authority of state or family.

Thanks to the bravery of my mother and my father, I managed to change the role that was prescribed for my life as a woman, which would have reduced my entire personality to that of a housework-performing wife. Naturally, my intellectual independence came at a price, including five court cases against me, and one against my daughter, the writer and poet, Dr Mona Helmi, only because she included her mother's name in her signature at the end of one of her poems (as a tribute to mothers on Mother's Day). But my parents' words remain carved in my mind since childhood: 'No matter how high the price of independence, it's not as high as that of submission and slavery.'

A Letter from a Woman Prisoner

A few days ago, I got hold of a newspaper. Their photograph was on the front page. The girl's thick wavy black hair, like mine before it started falling out, her features reminiscent of my mother's before she died, reminiscent of mine when I smiled, before I forgot how to smile. It's been six years since I looked in a mirror. They took away mirrors and pencils, since they were sharp instruments. Another prisoner had killed herself with a pencil.

I saw him in the photograph sitting like a lion perched in his lair, the coif of blond hair sitting on top of his head like a rooster's comb. His face glistened under the lights, his muscles probably vibrating with an aggressive energy, made more aggressive by the fact that instead of monstrous or predatory it appeared childlike and spontaneous.

The first time I saw a zebra in a primary school textbook, I thought it looked wilder than the lion. 'A lion only attacks when hungry. Some people attack with full bellies,' wrote my father in an article he published when I was nine years old. The 'dawn visitors' raided our home and took my father in his night clothes. His crime: infringement of the words of the 'Supreme Divine'. I never saw him again.

My mother warned me against committing the same crime. I didn't know exactly who the 'Supreme Divine' was, but I kept away from politics altogether. I graduated with distinction from the Faculty of Science and got a good job in a big corporation. One day in the month of March, I heard some of my former classmates talking about a women's march on International Women's Day. My mother said, 'Go, my daughter! And I'll come with you. Everyone is talking about empowering women. These are safe subjects that don't interfere with politics or touch the Supreme Divine.' My mother put on a new white dress and a green shawl and walked among the women with a confident step. She was a young woman again, enjoying herself and laughing. It was the first time I heard her laugh. I walked next to her, my hand in hers, chanting with the others: A WOMAN'S VOICE IS REVOLUTION!

Then suddenly the police were upon us. And men wearing *jalabiya*s and carrying sticks. My mother got hit on her head and fell to the ground in the middle of the road. My friends and I gathered around her, trying to tie the green scarf around her head to stop the bleeding. Another strike hit my head and I lost consciousness. When I came to, I was in a prison cell with my mother and some of the girls. My mother's head was still bleeding, and no one was helping. I was only half-conscious.

A few weeks after my mother was allowed to go home, she died. In prison, I was 'medically examined'. No idea what exactly they were examining. I wasn't brave enough to look at my body after they made me strip, especially not that area that had been off-limits since childhood, secured by the fear of sin. I stayed in my cell year after year, for six years, then I stopped thinking and I could relax.

I saw the photograph in the newspaper a few days ago. I was sitting cross-legged on the floor in front of a rusty plate holding the remnants of a lentil soup the colour of a baby's diarrhoea, and a piece of stale dust-covered bread. I dozed off, my head falling onto my chest like it happens to old people, falling asleep sitting up.

I saw my mother in her new white dress, untainted by blood. She was joyful like a child, laughing and singing with the others: 'A WOMAN'S VOICE IS REVOLUTION!' I said, 'But they told me that you died six years ago, Mum!' She smiled, 'They're all liars. I'm alive my daughter.' I asked, 'Have you been released from prison?' She said, 'Of course. Didn't you see me in the newspaper?' But I didn't see her face in the photograph. I must have spilled the lentil soup on the newspaper and smudged it.

His face was very clear, as if sculpted in stone. I remembered that I had seen him before, in other pictures and sculptures, going all the way back to Ramses I and Alexander and Bonaparte and the Sphinx who lost his nose to an invader's bullet. But bullet-proofing techniques have evolved, as have techniques in warfare and sculpting. An artist is capable of portraying Hitler and make him look like Jesus.

The face before me in the photograph kept changing, its features wavering and teetering on the edges of various impressions until any real distinctions were blurred out of existence, the tension between crude tyranny and defenceless insecurity sank deep under the skin, and only pure power rose to the surface.

My mother whispered to me, 'Sweetie, you should find a contact in the White House,' and then she was gone.

The Girl Outside the Court

The girl stood outside the gate, her *jilbab* stained with mud and blood, and pleaded with the guard to let her in. He told her she needed a permit.

She stood for a long time pressing her small child to her chest. It was cold, the girl sobbed and her baby screamed. She begged the guard to have mercy on her innocent child. The guard answered gruffly that the court gate could only be opened with a permit. Did she not have someone to write a permit for her and stamp it with the eagle seal?

'I have no one but God, sir,' she answered. Then, he advised her, she should go to heaven's gate – *that* is open to everyone and needs no permit. She asked him about the way to the gate of heaven. He scolded her for her ignorance and because she was young and alone, couldn't read and didn't know her right from her left.

The guard crossed his legs on his wooden bench, ate and drank, went to sleep and woke up.

The girl was still standing there, still holding her baby against her chest, still pleading.

The guard was surprised by her insistence. He started to feel sorry for her. She had come seeking justice like many others. The gate to the court, like the gate to heaven should be open to her and to all mothers.

He looked at her with her tattered clothes, her pale face,

her cracked feet, and thought that she almost reminded him of his late mother. He gave her his seat, allowing her to sit while he stood on his feet in the night, pacing back and forth to keep the blood flowing in his legs, and amused himself by talking to himself and singing in a tone that he tried to approximate to his mother's who used to sing for him when he was a child.

The girl sat on the backless bench, leaned her back against the wall, and moved her child from her chest to her knees.

The guard asked her about the baby's father. Her son didn't have a father. The guard shook his head and assured her in an even gruffer voice now that she couldn't enter through the court's doors until her child acquired a man's name, any man, even a murderer or a thief or a national traitor. By law, she could even use the name of a made-up father, as long as she paid the dues. 'What are the dues?' she asked. And the guard said that they were nothing compared to the lawyer's fee and expenses, the honour tax, and tips for clerks and cleaners. 'Is there no honour in the court without fees?' asked the girl. The guard replied, 'We have nothing to offer that doesn't cost money.'

Every day when it got dark, the girl would lie by the wall under the night's cover and hold her child to her, and in the morning she would resume standing by the gate. The guards alternated by day and by night, their faces changing while their uniforms and gruff voices remained the same. Some of them gave her their backless bench to sit on, then took it back when they saw her empty pockets or realised that her child had no father, real or imaginary. They grunted and turned away from her. She appealed to their love for their mothers, begged them to let her see the judge. They would say that no one could go in without a lawyer or a case file with papers and testimonies and seals and witnesses.

The guards got distracted by crowds of people entering and exiting the building, then sat scratching their mosquito bites and forgot about her. And the girl continued to plead and cry, until her eyes weakened and she could no longer tell day from night. But hope in a mother's heart is like an ever-burning star in the sky.

She saw a speck of light sparkle in the dark, behind the courthouse gate, and imagined that it was about to open like the gate to heaven: God would let it open and a voice in the horizon would call to her and call her son by her name, call all the sons and daughters by their mothers' names, and the gate to paradise would be wide open and she would enter with her son without needing a permit and God would say, 'Heaven lies under your feet and the feet of all mothers.'

Time passed while she slept holding her son, keeping him warm with her body and keeping herself warm with his. However long the night was, however long the dream, she always woke up and found instead of the fine green silk of paradise, nothing but the black walls of the court building, smeared with the blood of mothers and the faeces of their children. Something in her heart kept whispering: 'It can't be that this is a world without justice.' God knew her

son had a known father who had told her she was his love
and God was their witness, and after she gave birth to the
child, he had told her he had another love and told her to
go on her way.

The boy's nose resembled his father's. The girl told the
guard, 'Look, isn't this the same nose?' The guard laughed
until his vision was clouded by tears and said, 'The court
doesn't look at noses, girl. It looks at documents and
witness testimonies.' She said, 'God was our witness.' He
wiped his tears and said, 'God's testimony cannot file a
court case. You need a written document sealed with the
eagle stamp.'

A Girl's Death

The general prosecution didn't use to investigate the death of girls as a result of circumcision (FGM), despite the act being criminalised in 2008.

In June 2013, the child Soheir, 13 years old, died during a circumcision operation. Her father reported the doctor and accused him of negligence. A Ministry of Health inspector examined the girl's body and found signs of cauterisation in the genital area and reported that the cause of death was shock and sudden circulatory collapse. The prosecution started to question the father, who in turn withdrew his accusations against the doctor. The doctor denied having performed a circumcision and said the child had a dermal growth that he excised with a cauteriser, which the coroner confirmed. The doctor was only charged with medical negligence.

But in November 2013, the National Population Centre asked the General Prosecution Office to form a medical inquest committee. The doctor and the father were charged with involuntary manslaughter and referred to the court. In March 2014, the prosecution decided that the incident pertains to the offences of involuntary manslaughter and performing an FGM operation under criminal law. This was the first time FGM was criminally trialled since the 2008 amendments to the Child Act (1996) banning the practice, issued following the death of the child Bodour on 14 June 2007. In spite of medical and legal evasiveness, the doctor was sentenced to two years and a fine of 500 Egyptian pounds for involuntary manslaughter and three months for the offence of performing an FGM operation, setting a precedent in Egyptian law.

In 2016, following the death of another child, Mayar, in Suez, FGM was no longer considered a minor offence and became a felony.

Can We Not Even Wonder?

Where can we find the awareness necessary to unearth truths from under piles of inherited lies that prevail across the fields of history, politics, philosophy, religion, medicine, art, law, and ethics?

Where can the Egyptian mind find the ability to expose the cunning schemes that conceal injustice and physical and economic plunder under a veil of the spiritual and sacred?

What genius mind can decipher islamophobia, for instance, or the ISIS wars and sectarian rifts, to reveal hidden European and American agenda? Or penetrate the thick media fog around the Aqsa Mosque created by Israel to cover up the killing of Palestinians detained in its prisons and the building of more and more illegal settlements?

Is evil always linked to intelligence, shrewdness, and evolved mental skills?

Why do the power and wealth of states and individuals increase in proportion to their ability to lie and deceive?

Israel has become the most powerful country in the region, despite its crimes against humanity and its incessant violation of UN resolutions. The United States has become the most powerful country in the world, despite its known crimes and ongoing support of Israel.

Life experience has taught me that men and women who are most capable of deception become the wealthiest and climb highest in ranks. Yesterday I was invited to the house of an old friend who continues to write about democracy, while having remained close to rulers in all eras. He was never subjected to their tyranny, even if he sometimes opposed them, because he has always been good at evasion and justification, whichever side he takes. He considers hypocrisy a manner of social intelligence, so he wins everyone's friendship and is never found out. Even his wife knows nothing about his life outside the house. In times of crisis, he abandons his friends and watches as they are punished by the powers that be just for voicing their opinions.

I didn't hear from him when I lived in exile, when I was in prison, when I was targeted by *hisbah* trials or at any other time of adversity. Then, just recently, he invited me to his house in a posh neighbourhood. I didn't know why, but I told myself maybe the invitation would inspire a new article.

In the fancy villa, the table was laden with the most lavish foods, while waiters walked around carrying plates and trays. Spirits were served in silver bowls, holy verses were displayed in gold frames, the air was conditioned into a permanent spring, banishing the 43 degrees Celsius weather outside the large glass windows through which the garden and the trees could be admired.

I remembered Shukri Bey's villa from my childhood. I grew up between two different social classes: my father's poor village family were more humane and honest, despite their grimy *jalabiya*s, than my mother's rich family, despite their ironed suits and gleaming dresses. I instinctively aligned myself with my father's family, who stood with the revolution against the colonisers, the king, the Brotherhood, and the rich upper classes that accused Nasser of communism (ignoring the fact that he sentenced communists to ten years of prison with hard labour).

The ruling classes inherited their cunning and deception from colonialists, old and new, and learned to repeat well-polished words such as 'democracy'. Israel became the only democratic country in the region, and the United States the haven of democracy on earth.

Donald Trump's administration is working with some congress members to issue a law that would prevent American citizens from partaking in a civil society movement boycotting Israeli settlements' products grown or made on occupied Palestinian territories. The reality of American democracy is revealed when it turns against its own people and takes away their rights to express themselves against injustice and racist oppression.

For years, Israel has repeatedly ignored the warnings of the UN Security Council and refused to implement UN resolutions. Instead of punishment, when it bombed Iraq and Syria, it received even more financial aid and advanced chemical and nuclear weapons. While all the Arab nations, and Palestinians are not an exception, have been punished with murder, wars, division, and terrorism. Pro-Palestinian rulers like Gaddafi and Saddam Hussein were killed for exercising tyranny and dictatorship, while others who abandoned their people and collaborated with American-Israeli colonialism were rewarded.

Today, could the Egyptian and Arab intelligentsia take part in campaigns to boycott Israel? Instead of, say, campaigning against Nasser? Or building religious fatwa kiosks and calling for prayers at the Aqsa Mosque? Or veiling young girls and circumcising them? Or indulging in polygamy or marrying off minors?

Don't the Egyptian and Arab elites ask themselves questions such as why campaigns to boycott Israeli products always start outside the Arab world?

Those civil society activists, women and men, of multiple cultures and religions or – in most cases – no religion at all, believe in humanity, justice, dignity, freedom, and equality among all people regardless of religion, gender, or nationality, and fight for our rights more than we do. Isn't this something that calls for shame? Or consideration? Or at least wonder?

Not an Ideal Woman

I'm going to write about her – not about Donald Trump, Angela Merkel, Sadat, Mubarak, Obama, Clinton, Daesh, the Brotherhood or any of the others who possess weapons, power or wealth, but about her. Let the others have their writers, journalists, and media people who orbit them like moths orbit a flame in the dark.

I'll write about her anonymous name and body. She came to me many years ago, asking to work as a cleaner in my home to provide for her two children. She said, 'I'm Samira. We were in primary school together. Don't you remember me?'

In a flash, her bright childhood features emerged from behind the extinguished drooping face. She was the cleverest girl in class. Then she suddenly dropped out. Her father locked her up and forced her to marry. Her husband later divorced her, orally, and married another. She was on the street with her son and her daughter. She did the rounds in the courts, trying to get the divorce registered and obtain child support. The father refused to acknowledge the daughter so she would be excluded from his inheritance. The mother didn't have the money for lawyers' fees. She had no one but God. But divine providence does not count in court.

Samira and her daughter started working as house

cleaners. Her son became a zero-hour contract labourer. He married a woman who also worked as a cleaner and had two sons. One was killed in Iraq. The other worked in Libya, got married and had two sons. One emigrated to Italy. The other got killed in the war against Daesh. Life went on.

Wrapped up in her black veil, she limps along the Ideal Mothers queue, her spirit broken, her body dissociated from her name, like it belongs to a stranger. I saw her yesterday: Samira, with her daughter or her granddaughter. Her expression hollow and stiff. She looked like she had been snuffed out. The mayor handed her a certificate with gold-illuminated letters. She didn't know how to read it.

When I started writing about women's issues in the mid-1950s, they said women's issues was a Western concept imported to weaken Muslims.

Over sixty years ago, having graduated from medical school, I began to revisit my study of medicine to link it with the study of history, philosophy, and the origins of the universe, in order to answer simple questions like: Why do we cut parts away from bodies of healthy children and call it circumcision? Why did the teacher strike out my mother's name when I wrote it next to my father's on my school copybook? Why was my mother forced to give up her dream of studying music, so that instead of writing symphonies she gave birth to nine children?

Why is a woman's life measured by her husband's and his children's achievements and not her own?

Why is the role of mother and wife imposed on her by both state and family?

Why is the 'model' woman chosen based on her womb and not her brain?

Why are thinkers revered if they are men and hated if they are women? As if thinking is an eccentricity for a woman, a disability.

These questions are impossible to answer without delving into a long arduous journey through history, sciences and religions, to untangle the historically contingent roots of patriarchal authority. The father's authority cannot be seen separately from the authority of the ruler or the ruling class. Hence, the enslavement and oppression of women and the poor continue, along with local and global wars, increase in the production of weapons of mass destruction, evolvement in tools of espionage, deception, pillage and colonialism.

The father lying to the mother in the nuclear family is but the first ring in a chain of bigger lies spoken between nation states.

Political lies are not separate from economic, religious, ethical and sexual lies – and national treason is not separate from family betrayals. A man spies on his wife just like the leaders of the most powerful states spy on each other. Strong armies continue to crush weaker countries and fathers continue to oppress women and children.

Despite all that, it's still women, especially poor women, who are expected to sacrifice themselves, their lives and the lives of their children, for the sake of the state.

To women and to the poor, the state offers nothing but oppression and poverty. While the rich and powerful live in luxury and bliss.

Why don't we ever – except in cases as rare as raindrops in the desert – see men and women of wealth and power among the parents of martyrs? Why are the morgues, whether at the time of revolution or clashes with internal or external invasions, only visited by down-trodden poverty-stricken mothers? Why are the courts filled with queues of divorced poor women fighting to get financial support or inheritance or even recognition of parentage for their children? Why are most laws in the Egyptian legal system based on secular tenets, except for family and personal status laws which still employ religion to control mothers and wives?

Religion, Women and Cinema

The first time I went to a cinema, it was during my child-hood. I went with my parents and older brother to watch the Egyptian film *Long Live Love*. My brother loved music and cinema, and used to skip the religion class to play oud and sing with his girlfriend Sophie. My mum liked the Egyptian actress and singer Layla Mourad. Dad said she looked like her and had the same beautiful voice. Mum dreamt of being an actress sauntering on the magic screen, adored by millions, not owned by one man whom she married after having seen him only from behind half-open shutters. I disliked the religion teacher because he preferred my brother, despite the fact that he climbed over the school's wall and ran from school to music and love, while I remained a prisoner of virtue and the wooden school desk, content with daydreams, playing music only in my bedroom like it was a secret affliction, seeing my dream to be a dancer as only that: an impossible dream. The question I have asked myself all my life is this: Why do children always prefer music and dancing to teachers and religion lessons?

Despite attempts to modernise religious thought, ongoing to this day, it has remained frozen in the stone age. Aren't most new religious scholars indistinguishable from their age-old predecessors in their conviction that a man can cast off his wife orally and without witnesses, with the same ease he would take off his shoes?

The day when children begin to like lessons in religion as much as they like music, cinema, and dancing, the day when a woman's honour and dignity are the same as a man's, only then would religious thought have become 'modernised'. Aren't the core truths of religion the same as the core truths of art, that is, love, beauty, honesty, freedom, virtue, dignity, health and happiness?

A recent book, *Wicked Cinema: Sex and Religion on Screen* by Daniel S. Cutrara, sets out to study the relationship between religion, women, and cinema. Cutrara is a lecturer at Texas University who used to be a priest, then left the church because of his love for cinema. In his book he analyses some of the imaginative films of the late twentieth century, including Martin Scorsese's *The Last Temptation of Christ* which examines the place of women and sexuality in the spiritual life of Christ, and Woody Allen's *Crimes and Misdemeanours* which depicts the tragedy in the life of a Jewish doctor who is torn between bodily desires and religious teachings. From Arab cinema, Cutrara looks at the film *Closed Doors* by Atef Hetata about a Muslim young man who is turned into a murderer in God's name by a terrorist religious group.

Creative cinema plays a part in exposing chronic contradictions between the spirit and the body, transforming the subconscious into a more humanely refined, higher level of consciousness, allowing the mind to understand duplicity in moral values and social hypocrisy and the endless battles between the sacred and the profane, the individual and the group. It also brings to light how political systems use natural human needs for food, security, love and sex as a means to achieve hegemony over the minds of the masses and to collect their money. Under different religions, most of the world is controlled by the same system: class-based patriarchy, defined by the laws of a capitalist market that trades in spirituality alongside everything else. The Jewish-Christian bloc in the United States attacked Allen's and Scorsese's films and accused them of blasphemy, but they couldn't ban them from being shown in the cinemas. On the contrary, the attacks played a part in increasing their circulation and they went on to win awards.

The Egyptian film *Closed Doors* won a number of awards when it premiered eighteen years ago, and was considered by critics to be an important film in the history of Egyptian cinema. It grappled with the question of global relevance contemporaneous to its time: Why and how would a human being turn into a murderer in the name of God?

The film brings to light the psychological factors, as well as the economic and educational, that could compel a young man to denounce those around him as infidels and cause a teenager to join an extremist religious group and disown his closest kin. It shows how his need for sex was used to turn him into a murderer through making him believe that beautiful virgins are waiting for him in the afterlife.

The film was attacked by terrorist groups that were at

the peak of their activity in Egypt. It only stayed in the cinemas for one week. But good art can refine morals and strike down the currents corrupting our youth's minds along with those who push young men towards violence and tempt them to consider women as properties to be exploited by men with no accountability.

Innovative cinema has the power to modernise religious thought. It permeates the conscious and unconscious and influences children and boys at early formative phases of their lives.

Absolute Certainty and the Virus of Doubt

Magda – everyone called her Maggie – was a theatre professor at New York University, who had emigrated from Egypt some years before, following a painful experience that she disclosed to no one. She was a recluse who lived alone in near-perfect isolation, concerned only with her work, her art, her lectures which many, including myself, were keen to attend. She knew a lot about Egyptian and international theatre and was respected by everyone, professors and students alike. She was young, not yet forty, had a shapely figure and attractive, very Egyptian features. Men flocked to her, holding banners of love or marriage, but she always turned them away graciously. We became friends, brought together by art and creativity and mutual fondness.

One day she told me, 'Everything is full of doubt, even love.'

She didn't enjoy teaching, especially not American students who had a tendency towards vivacity and loudness, while she was quiet by nature. One student whose name was Edouard caught her attention; he had a French-Indian background, was artistic and sensitive, deep-thinking and quiet. His classmates called him Daoud.

One hot summer day, she came over to my place when I

wasn't expecting her, looking unusually pale and nervous, and told me what had happened that same morning.

She was walking across the bridge at 8:30am, as was her habit on the way to her university office, when she saw something that stopped her in her tracks. Daoud was standing halfway across the bridge, his hands gripping the iron rail, his back turned towards her and his eyes fixed on the water running under the bridge. A grey denim jacket hung on his shoulder. She walked over and, without premeditation, reached out and touched his hand, as if she wanted to make sure he was really there and not just in her head. His fingers were ice-cold, despite New York's hot summer sun. He was startled by her touch, jumped as if woken from a trance or a deep sleep. Without warning, his feet were on the railing and in a split second he was in the water. She let out a sharp scream that no one in the speeding cars took notice of. People in New York City don't hear others screaming when they're in the safety of their tightly shut cars. And at that time of the morning, no one walked.

Daoud left nothing behind but the grey denim jacket which slid off his shoulder and landed at her feet. Her body bent by itself and her trembling fingers picked up the jacket. She held it like she was holding a piece of his body that had separated itself at the moment of jumping. She considered throwing the jacket into the water after him and continue on her way before anyone could see her, but she opened her handbag instead and put the jacket inside. Back at her home, she hung it on the coatrack and sat at a distance watching it, apprehensively like it might be holding a dead person. She couldn't keep it during the night. Her late grandmother's voice came back to tell her that the spirits of the dead returned at night.

She decided she was going to throw it in the rubbish bin at the back of the house. While placing the jacket in the black bin bag, she felt something in the top pocket. She pushed her hand in and pulled out a folded paper. She opened it and read the following lines written in pencil:

I apologise for missing your lecture yesterday. I had a sudden migraine and severe vertigo. I lay down on the bed to regain my balance, dozed off for a while, and dreamt I saw myself standing on the bridge thinking about ending my own life. I don't know where my will to live has gone these past days. Is it my love for you? My fear of losing you? Or is it that I never loved you and wish to escape? I don't believe in absolute certainty free of doubts. Everything is suspect, even love. I thought that love was the one exception capable of defeating doubt, but I have found that love is just like everything else. This truth is tormenting me. It is so painful it makes me wish for death. Love used to be the one thing that gave life meaning.

I was certain that I loved you and couldn't live without you. But that certainty didn't last long. Doubt began to infect my thoughts like an unknown virus, flowing stealthily in my veins. I tried to get rid of it, but it was futile. Will you forgive me?

Taleq, Professor!

She was a Professor of Economics at the university and called me ignorant when I wrote about women's issues. She would purse her lips in contempt and say, 'These are trivial issues, Nawal. History is shaped by economics.' I told tell her that women are half of the nation. We cannot liberate our economy without liberating women. Historically, the class system is part and parcel with the patriarchal system, and economy has been linked to gender and politics, to education and culture, to religion, etc... etc...

The professor didn't listen to me. By the late seventies, her husband became a theology scholar, one of the stars of the new 'faith & science' programmes. She began linking economics with sharia laws, and Islamic banks with capitalist open-door policies. She wore a head turban which evolved into a hijab without giving up her full make-up and dark-red lipstick. Then by the late eighties, her eyes – black with kohl – began peering out of the holes of a niqab; the rest of her face and body hid behind a thick black fabric that, in the words of religious scholars, did not show or hint at what was underneath it. But her voice remained loud and her tongue sharp, ringing everywhere and attacking anyone who dared speak about women's liberation or any change in the double-standard marriage and parentage laws, which give men absolute authority and absolve them from any responsibility towards their wives and children, free of legal controls, and letting young women alone carry the consequences of the recklessness of lecherous men.

We punish the weak victim and exonerate the powerful perpetrator under the rubric of the law. Since the beginning of written history, all contracts have been recorded in writing, from the selling and buying of cattle and property to marriage contracts and divorce papers. Written notarised law reigns in all human dealings in all countries of the world, including Tunisia, Morocco, Indonesia, Malaysia, all the way to the far-flung corners of the earth. Everywhere except in our homeland, where the Egyptian man can, until this day, stretch out his limbs, yawn and exhale the air from his chest with a booming '*Taleq!*' and that's all he needs to do for his wife and children to be displaced from their home.

Egypt is at the tail end of international rankings when it comes to corruption and high divorce rates. Recently, the president of the state called for a system that requires divorce to be registered at a marriage notary office. But the Economics Professor protested: 'The economy is the real problem here! Demands to notarise divorce pronouncements bring nothing but trouble and social sedition. Spoken divorce is stipulated for in the religious texts, and haven't we had enough with Susanne Mubarak's law obliging a husband to notify his first wife before he marries the second? Doesn't that contradict Islamic law? A man should have absolute freedom to divorce or take

multiple wives, and a pious woman should do nothing but
submit to the will of God. Susanne's Law has enabled the
spread of immorality, pushing men to resort to clandestine marriage in order to wed young women behind the
government's back. God and his prophet have laid down
the laws for us, and we shouldn't forbid what God and
the prophet have sanctioned. Spoken divorce has, in fact,
spread because of poverty, the rise in prices and the fall of
the economy. Moral chaos has also been on the increase
since the January Revolution, which broke down the fear
barriers so that revolutionary girls went around shamelessly exercising freedoms, spreading Western ideas which
contradict with our Eastern values and honoured sharia.'

Those were some of the pronouncements of the economics professor, and they angered many women and
men – those who do not want to divorce their wives with
one word or practise polygyny. The economics professor's
niqab had, since the 30 June Revolution and the ousting of
the Muslim Brotherhood government, once again shrunk
to a turban. I kept getting phone calls from members of
feminist organisations, one of whom shouted at me, 'She's
speaking nonsense, this economist! You have to answer,
Nawal!' I was astonished. Where is the feminist movement? I wondered. There are hundreds, if not thousands,
of governmental and non-governmental women's organisations. Why doesn't their collective voice rise up, not just
in favour of notarising divorce with a marriage clerk or a
judge, but in favour of a whole new personal status law
compatible with the constitution, an integrated civil law

that achieves justice and full equality among all Egyptian citizens.

Millions of women all around the world went out in massive demonstrations against the new American president Donald Trump and his racist, classist, patriarchal policies which target women, blacks, immigrants, and the poor. An organised, well-informed women's movement is a force to be reckoned with. It can topple thrones and change laws, especially when united with the poor, with men, youth and children. No? 'Yes,' she said.

Then this morning her voice greeted me again on the phone. 'You won't believe this, Nawal! Yesterday, the economics professor's husband divorced her! Now she's really keen to organise a protest against unregulated divorce.'

Hercules and Antaeus

I sat on the stone cliff and watched the thin line between the waters of the Mediterranean Sea and the Atlantic Ocean, separating Spain from the coastal mountains of Morocco. At Monouf Primary School, they taught us that this was the Strait of Gibraltar. In my childhood's mind's eye, I saw it as a shiny white hair that cuts across the blackness of two continents. In all my visits to Tangier, I have to walk along the coast to the very edge, where the sea and the ocean meet. Fancying myself a Zarqaʻ al-Yamama, I close my eyes and open them to see Spain, just fourteen kilometres away, fifteen minutes by boat.

I was invited to attend the Twiza arts and literature festival (Festival Méditerranéen de la Culture Amazighe) which takes place every summer in Tangier, the city that we find eternalised in the words of the Moroccan writer Mohamed Choukri, who lived and died there, thus: 'Skies in which dimensions merge and time and space interweave.'

Tangier transcends all boundaries and is not subject to the usual human classifications. All ethnicities, civilisations, colours, languages, religions, nationalities and cultures co-exist here. Of all the languages known in this land – Amazighi, Ancient Egyptian, Greek, Phoenician, Latin, Arabic, Spanish, French, English and Italian

– Amazighi is the oldest. I was accompanied by one of the festival organisers, Mohamed Aznaki, a young man who is very passionate about Amazighi history. He recounted to me four thousand years of Tangier's history. He was very proud that Berber has become an official language alongside Arabic in Morocco. We were also accompanied by a young woman called Nawal al-Zayani, the festival's writer in residence, who in her insubordination to authority reminded me of my friend, the Moroccan writer Fatima Mernissi who used to take me to Tangier, Asilah, and Fez, and invite me to panels at Mohammed V University in Rabat, and to walks around the market and mint-tea drinking sessions at the cafés.

The festival hall in Tangier was full, mostly with young men and women from around Morocco who had come and brought with them so much enthusiasm for listening and debating. Many of them had read my writings in Arabic, French or Spanish – generations from the past five decades following what I write on paper or on the internet. At least fifty-five of my books are now available online for free, for all the readers who can't buy books, since the price of books has gone up like everything else. It's an example of how the human mind with its amazing creative abilities can conquer time and space. The only regrettable thing is that Arab countries have hardly contributed to the technology that makes this possible.

Public demonstrations were raging in Morocco. Not far from Tangier, El Hoceima echoed with chants against the government and corruption. I was told these protests were only aimed at the government and not the king. In the eyes of Moroccans, the king is not accountable for evil but only for good. On the mountain I saw the three words which have been engraved since the ruling family came to power: Allah, Homeland, King. In the annual royal address, the king repeats this phrase: 'In Morocco, politics and religion only come together in my person, the prince of the faithful.'

After the conquest of Granada, many Spanish Muslims left for Morocco and settled in Tangier. It's a multi-ethnic, multicultural city where singularity of creed has no place and everyone is welcome regardless of religion, race, nationality, language, etc. Tangier was called Tingis after the wife of Antaeus in Greek mythology. According to a mix of Greek, Roman, and Berber legends, Hercules defeated Antaeus and claimed both Tingis the woman and Tingis the city, reigning over the land and its riches. Millions of tourists every year gather to see the Cave of Hercules in Tangier, as they would with the Great Pyramid of Giza during the golden age of tourism in Egypt. Although I usually try to not go where tourists are, I did visit the cave. My Moroccan friends recommended that I see it and witness the twelve labours of Hercules. I imagined those labours were heroic acts, but then found out that they consisted of murder and ISIS-style beheadings. It was class-based patriarchy again, reigning over humanity since the age of slavery until today. Is Hercules any different from the rulers of the modern or post-modern world who do not cease from running after money and power, assaulting others and leaving bloodshed in their wake?

Defamation of Religion and *Al-Gama'a* in Ramadan

The title of the book is *Blasphemy in Egypt*. The first part, titled 'Blasphemy and A Defence of Islam', is written by Magdi Khalil; the second, by Hamdi al-Assiouti, discusses blasphemy laws in Egypt. This is a serious study of law, religion, society, politics and history. It contains documents from the most significant court cases of blasphemy in the past hundred years, twenty-three cases in total against the following individuals (in rough chronological order): Sheikh Ali Abdel Raziq, Ismail Adham, Taha Hussein, Khaled Mohamed Khaled, Mahmoud al-Sharqawi, Louis Awad, Alaa Hamed, Nasr Hamed Abu Zayd, Nawal El Saadawi, Hassan Hanafi, Sayyid al-Qemani, Helmi Salem, Ahmed Abdel Muti Hijazi, Adel Imam, Nader Galal, Oussama Fawzi, Lenin el-Ramli, Wahid Hamed, Mohammad Fadel, Ibrahim Eissa, Naguib Sawiris, Alber Saber Ayad, Beshoy Kamil Kamel.

The book looks into the roots of socio-political religious intimidation. It exposes the lie of Islamophobia in the West, the Euro-American-Israeli deception, how the religiously extremist militarily armed political Islamist movements were bolstered by the West to weaken those nations struggling against external colonialism and internal exploitation, to suppress freethinkers and innovators

– except for government-trained ones – and how anti-terrorism laws were introduced to advance the agendas of external colonialism and internal totalitarianism. How the criminalisation of religious blasphemy entered into Egypt's criminal law, and how the language of law became elusive and cryptic, difficult even for specialists to clearly decode let alone the rest of the population pushed into ignorance by fatwas and by the new preachers that became TV stars, making huge fortunes off the religion and fatwa business. And how educational institutions, both public and private, have become tools for misguidance, imposing veils on minds before heads, oppressing the minds and bodies of women in the name of God and God's prophet.

In the eighties, Sheikh Metwali al-Sharaawi led a vicious campaign against intellectuals and freedom of expression. He claimed to be working on Allah's behalf, so anyone disagreeing with him would be working for the devil. I joined the ranks of infidels just for criticising his following statement: 'Those who listen to Beethoven before sleep instead of the Qur'an will not go to heaven,' and of his claim that female circumcision and women's hijab are Muslim duties necessary to safeguard morality. I exposed the error of this idea from medical, social, and ethical angles.

The tenth document included in the book cited above presents the case brought against me, which almost led to stripping me of my Egyptian citizenship for a fictional play I wrote.

How is it possible to take imagination to court? Or for

an Egyptian writer to lose her citizenship just for using her imagination? I inherited my Egyptian-ness from my Ancient Egyptian grandmothers, five thousand years if not longer before the advent of Islam. The first article of the Egyptian constitution lays down the principle of citizenship; how can it be negated by the second article that decrees Islam as the religion of the state?

The foundation of the constitution, and the international convention of political and civil rights, are premised on the idea that every human being possesses freedom of thought, spirit and religion, hence full liberty to decide their own religion and beliefs. How can the constitution then impose Islam on all Egyptians?

Well, laws and constitutions, the world over, obey the rules of power and violence, not the command of justice. Anything could be prescribed by the state in the name of security, or by the United States or Israel for less powerful countries in the name of democracy. Just like a man can do to a woman whatever he fancies in the name of God.

Despite the bloodshed they caused, the Muslim Brotherhood occupied large parts of the minds of Egyptians during the month of Ramadan, as members of the intelligentsia fell over each other writing about the TV series produced about the group. These shows spread neurosis and bigotry among the people. Meanwhile, endless advertising eats away at their hearts and minds. The free market uses women's bodies, making them dance around half-naked before eyes that are deprived of the essentials of life, in order to promote the most inessential of products. Who needs lipstick for lips cracked from lack of clean drinking water, or nail polish for hands dried from scrubbing floors?

The month of Ramadan has become a prison and a burden, its TV shows draining the already starved spirits, profitable only for a minority of commercial entertainment professionals, each one of whom earn enough to feed three million street children for twenty years. Nothing eased the misery of the month except demonstrations in Germany against ruthless capitalism and globalisation, in the face of representatives of a handful of greedy countries gathered in Hamburg to plot the world's route to ruin and poverty and ignorance and disease and environmental contamination. Arab countries fall like dominoes, while Israel keeps winning, its women armed and trained in nuclear and chemical warfare, and our women sinking under the flood of hijab and niqab. Or else, paraded in TV series to entertain Ramadan fasters or to sell halal products in the free market.

Reading Patriarchy in Egyptian History

The year five thousand BCE. The goddess Nut leaves a written will to her daughter Isis in which she says: 'I do not advise my daughter who will inherit my throne to draw her authority from divine sanctity. I advise her instead to be wise, merciful, and just.'

The European colonialist historians, however, erased the trailblazing philosophy of Ancient Egypt to claim that philosophy began in Greece. They propagated the idea that the old Egyptian culture was built on superstitions. This idea, which stands in contradiction to history, was picked up by intellectuals influenced by European thought and was part of the Egyptian school curriculum for several generations, as summed up in a book by an Egyptian philosopher. I remember that, forty years ago, I wrote an article in *Al-Ahram* newspaper criticising this claim, then the newspaper published a debate between me and said philosopher who denied the existence of Ancient Egyptian philosophy, let alone one led by women.

In the mid-1980s, a play written by Tawfiq al-Hakim and titled *Isis* had the main conflict all happening between male characters, and Isis only appeared as the wife of Osiris. Although history stresses that Isis's role in philosophy, politics and education was more extensive than her husband's, that it was in fact she who taught him about philosophy, medicine, agriculture, writing and the arts. Tawfiq al-Hakim laughed and said, 'Of course my view would be masculinist because I'm a man. Why don't you write the play from a feminist point of view?' I said, 'I'll write it based on historical facts, neither masculinist nor feminist.' And I wrote the play, just one year after al-Hakim's and published it in a book called *Isis* because it was banned by the authorities from appearing on stage, although Karam Mattawa wanted to direct it. The censorship report said that the play contained a transgression against the sacredness of divinity, which is the age-old accusation against creativity, in the West as well as in the East, and one of the first reasons behind violence and war and murder in the name of the gods throughout eras.

Philosophy and religious belief are rarely separate. Philosophy as a field has always constituted a methodology for theoretical research to prove a predetermined idea; in contradiction to its supposed objective, which is to clarify a truth not previously known. Yet most philosophers, with the exception of a few from the dialectic materialist school, fall into this trap. Ancient Egyptian philosophy, however, did not have this blind spot, as it took for its foundation justice and mercy, not divine sanctity.

The old manner of slavery, that is the class-based patriarchal order, has produced injustice and violence and feudal systems, which then evolved into capitalist systems, old and new, and spawned colonial, terrorist, political, military, and religious organisations, killing in the name of God. Doesn't Israel kill Palestinians and occupy their land in the name of a divine promise?

Recently in Egypt there's been a movement to revive the old Egyptian civilisation, trying to unearth the deep roots of Egyptian culture and its many tributaries extending to the depths of all interlinked episodes of Egypt's history. There is little variation between old Egyptian philosophy and other philosophies and religions, earthly or heavenly, that came after, including Judaism, Christianity and Islam. But some of the proponents of the revivalist movement want to isolate Egypt from its geopolitical environment, from its present and future, under the banner of a revered past. But the past, present, and future are rings in a continuous and tightly-woven chain, in whose composition awareness and knowledge accumulate, and from which the power and creativity of nations and individuals emanate.

No doubt the crimes of Daesh and their ilk have distorted the image of Arabs and Muslims. Yet history tells us that the crimes of Arabs are not worse than those of Americans, Israelis and Europeans, and that the blood that has been shed in the name of Judaism and Christianity is not less in quantity than that shed in the name of Islam.

The struggle continues between philosophers and thinkers according to their political and religious leanings and their class interests. But they converge in their masculinist view of history. Which is why the names of female intellectuals are erased or marginalised. That is exactly what happened to the Egyptian Isis, whose philosophical influence stretched from Egypt to Greece.

We must study our ancient history with a rational, scientific approach, devoid of over- or understatements, taking care not to bury the pioneering women philosophers who placed justice, equality and mercy above divine sanctity, in order to defeat the terrorist wars that are waged in the name of religion.

Psychiatry and Atheism

Most of my fellow medical students in the mid-fifties of the past century wanted to specialise as surgeons. They held the view that surgery entails a precise diagnosis followed by the excision of the diseased part from the body. The character of a surgeon is as precise and exacting as the tip of a scalpel. It knows no hesitation or ambiguity. It's also narcissistic and hubristic to the point of self-worship, rigidly biased in favour of one's own beliefs, and single-minded, intolerant of criticism and debate.

I worked in surgery for a few years, then quit before the scalpel in my hand found its way against the neck of the chief surgeon at the hospital where I worked. He treated the younger medics as if they were slaves on his country estate. And he did of course have a country estate. It was one of the five pillars of the dream: private clinic, car, apartment building, country house, trophy wife. In the end, my self-respect won over my love of surgery and I switched to other branches of medicine.

But the culture in those fields wasn't much better, and the work was less precise. Psychiatry, for instance, wasn't considered a real science at all. It was seen as a form of charlatanism, tackling mysterious symptoms with unknown causes, just like palm reading or tea-leaf divination. A psychiatrist was usually low on clients, had to use public transport like the rest of us or, at best, drove a locally manufactured Ramses car. Then suddenly there were rapid changes in Egyptian society. The economic open-door policies of the seventies, coupled with intellectual isolationism, brought faith and lack thereof into the midst of the commodities of the open market and the speculations of the stock exchange. Exported goods prevailed, and the market was flooded with exported prayer beads and veils for women. Money piled up in the safes of the fat cats: the leaders and businessmen. The gap between the rich and the poor widened, and with it the range of socioeconomic problems and disorders. The real causes of those issues were covered up in the media and passed as psychological and moral disorders, with the psychiatrists lining up to offer their diagnosis: a chemical imbalance in the brain and hormones, possibly triggered by frustration due to class-envy or atheism. Lack of faith must be the problem. One must be content with one's lot. Wealth is rationed by the creator among his creations, as our believer president said on the radio. Atheism could also be a result of failing to adapt to reality, helplessness in the face of impossible dreams, or a variety of phobias and fears. The poor feared increased poverty, and the rich feared a revolution. Stability had to be ensured by furthering political and religious oppression. So the authorities relied on preachers and men of religion to warn against God's punishment, and on psychiatrists and psychotherapists to warn against the consequences of rebelling against patriarchal authority, whether in the family or the state.

Preachers and psychotherapists thrived on fear and
anxiety. Sermons about torture after death and the demons
that visit a sinner's grave spread alongside prescriptions of
anti-depressant and hormone-boosting drugs to encour-
age happiness, love and faith. That's how a class of elite
preachers, televangelists, and psychiatrists were created.
They owned money and property and became media stars.

On New Year's Eve, just a few days ago, there was a distinguished sheikh on television, speaking about the 'new
phenomenon of atheism' as a foreign masonic conspiracy
against Islam. He was followed by a distinguished psychiatrist who considered atheism a mental health problem,
which could affect the youth for any of the following
reasons: the lack religious deterrents, a decline in manners
following the January Revolution, the absence of patriarchal authority because the father works in the Gulf, the
absence of maternal care because women are distracted
from their familial duties by work or personal ambitions.
The psychiatrist went on to analyse the common psychology of an atheist, declaring that he or she would have a
hysterical or paranoid personality, would be obsessive
compulsive, rebellious and disdainful towards patriarchal or divine rule, tending towards doubt and questioning and disagreement just to stand out and be seen, might
also suffer from schizophrenia or any host of psychotic or
neurotic disorders.

I had in my company that night a group of young men
and women who had taken part in the January Revolution.
All were of sound mental and physical health and most

were leaders or innovators in a number of diverse fields. They laughed as they listened to the distinguished psychiatrist, who had wilfully ignored all scientific and artistic inventions and creations, everything from electricity to computers, from cinema to symphonies, all the products of creative rebellious minds that started out doubting and questioning. Many nations, East and West, flourished and found their place on top of the world without sharing the religion or ideology that our experts assert as basic conditions of success. We often talk about modernising religious discourse. Closely tied with that but not talked about as much are the discourses of psychiatry and psychotherapy which should also be modernised.

Economics, Sex and Personal Status Law

No matter how many billions they make in the free market, how much caviar they eat, spirits they imbibe, how many wives and mistresses they own, the dormant historical fear of women and slaves revolting never leaves them.

In this century, the twenty-first, revolutions have been erupting here and there. The historical fear of poverty and suffering and of mass migration has resurfaced. One can no longer hear the voices of the free economy defenders. Their voices have been drowned by the voices of those who demand state intervention to curb private-sector greed and control competition, whether in sex trafficking, stock exchange, illicit drug trade, arms trade, cosmetics businesses, or espionage.

The sex trade market is no different from arms trade, drug trafficking, or currency exchange – it's all part of the free market, which thrives on fraud and deception. Money laundering plays a role in camouflaging war as a peace process, and drug and sex trafficking as individual freedom.

Justice is mostly nowhere to be found, and where it is found, it applies double standards. Justice can only flourish in a humane society that raises children to love justice and honesty more than money, power and sex. That is what we miss in a class-based patriarchal society and a market built on profiteering at any price – if you oppose it, your fate is failure and disappearance.

In a market based on the ethos of hunter and prey, the forbidden fruit is always sweeter. The more difficult to obtain, the higher the price of the prey. Trading in illegal goods is more profitable than anything else in this jungle. So many are horrified at the idea of state intervention to control the market, whether in economy or sex or in any other realm. They panic if the state intervenes in the private sector, claiming that what is private is separate from what is public, that state intervention never succeeded in other countries, and that socialist planning failed elsewhere – which is a media lie, because planning is only a tool for actual implementation, just like a pen is a tool for writing the honest truth or for spreading lies, and a knife is a tool for cutting cakes or severing heads.

The increase in national debt and the hike in the dollar exchange rate are some of the diseases of the market which strike Egypt's economy at its core. Egypt's annual imports reach more than sixty billion dollars, mostly spent on luxury goods – caviar, lipsticks, nail polish – or essential produce that could easily be grown locally, like beans. The market is designed to serve no one but a handful of rich businessmen at home and abroad.

In the sex trade of the free market, powerful males prey on young girls and poor women. Governments abandon their responsibilities towards one half of society – i.e. women – under the pretence of protecting personal freedom or separating the public from the private. Men have freedoms that women don't have. Men are not held accountable for what they do in the public sphere, because they own a private sphere, wife included, where they are not held accountable either. We live lives based on duplicity in a society built on duplicity, everyone carrying out in private what they deny and condemn in public.

Since the two revolutions of January 2011 and June 2013 in Egypt, the Egyptian constitution declares the secularity of Egyptian laws, and decrees that all citizens are equal in rights and duties regardless of religion or gender. Personal status and family laws, however, continue to follow the principals of Islam or Christianity or Judaism as the main source of legislation for the different religious groups. Private affairs remain separate from public affairs. Why? Because the exploitation of women requires such separation. Under the pretence of values, tradition, and religious law, women remain sex objects in the free patriarchal market.

How Costly is the Service of Religion?

In a meeting held with press reporters on 22 October 2016, the prime minister of Egypt declared that the national budget was 930 billion Egyptian pounds, and that 292 billion out of that is spent in the service of religion – meanwhile ignoring salaries, health, education, subsidy of essential goods, and other national services. This means that 'the service of religion' takes one third of the national budget alone.

Does it make sense to spend nearly EGP 300 billion in the service of religion, in a country drowning in economic crises, loans and aid, external and internal debt? All the while increasing that debt by accepting even bigger loans?

Doesn't God reside in the hearts of his worshippers? He doesn't need all that massive spending to build or restore houses of worship, pay the high fees of preachers and ser-monisers, reprint and distribute books of religion and doctrine.

My grandmother used to say: 'What the home needs should be denied to the mosque!' She would admonish her husband if he donated to the mosque the few coins she earned from selling the product of her small fields. She made a hole in the wall of the house where she hid the money needed for food, her children's education, and other requirements. Luckily, when her husband died, she was still a strong young woman capable of working and producing and providing for the family.

The mayor of her village used to accuse her of being ignorant of religion because she didn't read the Qur'an. She would reply: 'Work is worship.' Then she would recount the story of a group of people who told the prophet about a man who prayed all day and all night. The prophet asked, 'Who feeds that man's children?' The group replied, 'We all do.' So he said, 'You are all better than him.'

The majority of women in my village had this organic inherited wisdom which extends back in Egyptian history to the goddesses of wisdom, knowledge, and justice: Nut, Isis, and Maat.

Marriage based on mutual consent and separation based on mutual consent used to be practised in Egypt over seven thousand years ago. It was endorsed by Maat, the symbol of instinctive human justice, before laws were established for marriage and divorce, and before any of the Abrahamic religions appeared.

At the same time, Islamophobia is one of the clever weapons of colonialism, which follows this principle: intimidate people in the West with Islamist terrorism; spread fatwas that indict freethinkers, and deliver outlandish sermons on camel's urine, breastfeeding adults or how something as insignificant as an ant's behind might arouse a fasting man... Top all that with the Azhar resisting the *takfir* (excommunication) of Daesh, despite not holding back when it came to dozens of innovators and intellectuals; the most well-known Muslim preacher, Sheikh Yusuf al-Qaradawi, allocating an entire episode of his *Al-Jazirah* programme 'Sharia and Life' to discuss sexual relations between men and women; terrorising anyone who criticises Islam and not condemning al-Qaeda and Daesh or declaring their followers apostates, thereby opening the way for armed Islamic forces to multiply; obstructing the assimilation of Muslims in the West; encouraging the hijab in the name of personal choice and freedom of religion; the commission on religious freedom going around reviving customs that divide the nation according to religious sects: Shia, Sunni, Sufi, Salafi, Qur'anic; encouraging sedition between Muslims and Christians; stoking frustration among young Muslims in the West to isolate them and push them towards Daesh; justifying murders committed in the name of religion to absolve Islam and strike Muslims in one move; and barricading Muslims within a Muslim identity, so that the Islamic identity prevails over scientific and secular contributions.

Islamophobia is a political weapon more dangerous than military warfare. New colonialism no longer occupies the land with brigades and guns – it's much cheaper to destroy minds than to take over the land and the economy and everything else.

'Petrol Islam'... 'Islam is the answer'... 'Islam is in danger'... 'The danger of Islam for non-Muslims'...

Memories in the Mother Tongue

Before I visited any other African country, I had travelled from my city, Cairo, to most countries in the world, despite the fact that Egypt is planted in Africa – there we are born, there we live, and in its deep belly we are buried, our cultural and material roots, and the headwaters of our river Nile spreading out into its heart.

But our eyes were always looking north, towards the pillagers and oppressors in Europe and America, while our backs were turned to our very selves in Africa and the south.

What a double oppression this is, when a person turns her back on herself, when she is ashamed of her dark or black complexion and conceals it under whitening products. Women are often ashamed of their very womanhood, treating their faces as a sin that must be covered under a niqab.

The colonialist slavery system abused women and Africans and the poor, exploiting our economic resources and the wealth of our heritage which reaches back to before history had begun. They exhausted our material and cultural treasures, those that were buried deep underground, and those that stand tall above ground to this day, like the pyramids and obelisks and statues that the world still flocks down to see.

But the biggest colonial form of abuse was the arrow that white men aimed straight into the hearts of African people, so that their Africanness itself became a thing to be ashamed of, their blackness a seal of slavery.

My travels in Africa came relatively later in life. In the late seventies, when I was a consultant on the UN Economic Commission for Africa, I was based in Addis Ababa, but my work meant I had to travel to all of Africa's countries, on trips short and long, which were not enough for me to get to the heart of the vast ancient continent, but were enough to provide me with an opportunity to go deeper into my own heart and recognise myself as an African.

The primary manifestation of my Africanness is my dark skin. So that I can walk in the streets of Ethiopia, Uganda, or South Africa, and no one would notice that I was a stranger. That didn't immediately fill me with joy. You see, I had internalised – since childhood – a longing to be, as my maternal grandmother would put it, as white as cream. I had understood, pretty much since I was born, two indisputable truths: one was that I was 'a girl' and different from my brother, and two, that I was 'dark-skinned' and not 'white' like my mother. With these truths came an important realisation: that these two characteristics alone, without the addition of any other 'flaws', were enough to doom my future to failure.

The only qualification a girl needed in order to have a decent future was physical beauty, or at least a light complexion, like the Ottoman Turks who used to rule

the country. My maternal grandmother, who came from
a Turkish background, used to call me Werwer after a
woman slave on her grandfather's estate in Istanbul.

I understood since childhood that my skin was the
same colour as that of slaves, and I took to hiding it with
a light foundation powder that my maternal aunt Nemat
used to buy from the nearby pharmacy, along with whitening creams and blackening kohl. Hiding my real face
was the first step towards achieving correct beauty. But,
strangely enough, buried in a hidden corner at the core
of my consciousness, the same corner where the mother
tongue resides, was the deep knowledge that I was beautiful, positively the most beautiful girl there was, and my
brown skin, the colour of the Nile mud, was the prettiest
skin in the entire universe. That is my truth that I have
always – secretly – been proud of, the truest love I have
known.

That's how, as I got older, I became braver about facing
the world with a face washed from all make-up, feeling
more and more comfortable in my skin, and at home with
my body and my self. At home also with my Black African
friends. So much so that, to my surprise, I found myself
falling for a Senegalese man on my first visit to Dakar.
My childhood self used to run screaming at the sight of a
black person.

The coasts and mountains I saw in Africa were magical.
The peak of Kilimanjaro was for me grander than the
Himalayas or the Swiss mountains. Victoria Lake and the
Nile headwaters in Uganda have called to me like the sirens

in stories. African art, African cinema, dance, and music touch my very core. But my real passion became African literature, produced by men and women writers who have gained worldly fame with their authentic creativity.

Egypt too is on her way back into the embrace of her African mother, after a long period of being forcibly estranged from her and left to be or not to be in the undefined haziness hanging between two continents that the pillaging colonisers have labelled 'the Middle East'.

No Objectivity in a Violent World

I always choose to fly with EgyptAir, because of how delicately their pilots touch down when landing. They don't pound the ground violently like other pilots do, with the force of aggressors, in a way reminiscent of how brute masculinity treats a female body, viewing it as a land to be penetrated with an axe and battered with fertilisers before the seeds are sown to grow produce and progeny.

Earlier this month I got to know Egypt better during a visit to Sfax in Tunisia. Sometimes you need to get away from the homeland to see it more clearly. The Tunisian revolution got rid of the head of the regime, just like the Egyptian revolution did, but the structure of the regime lingered on, stable and rooted deep in the state with its institutions, laws, businesses and organisations. They continue with the smuggling, tax evasions, pillaging of state-owned land, suspect external relations, and old and new dollhouse political parties. Though the latter seem to have all dropped like autumn leaves, with the exception of the Salafi Party, still rising, still subsidised by dollars and veils and beards, still trying to bring back the age of bondwomen and wooden clogs and to legalise polygamy which is currently prohibited by Tunisian law. Money facilitates the spreading of fatwas and corruption, flooding the media and arts and Ramadan series with sex and violence, and commercials that harm national industries and favour stock market speculations, foreign investment, the world bank and IMF loans.

After Sfax, I was invited to Jebiniana, one of the most progressive places in Tunisia. It has a history of struggle against external and internal occupation. During a dialogue with hundreds of the village people, a young woman said to me: 'We heard that some of the women parliamentarians in Egypt support polygamy under the slogan "my husband, your husband".'

I said that I hadn't heard of that slogan which does not make sense to any woman with dignity and intelligence.

In Tunisia I met many examples of great women and men. I also witnessed many of the same issues that I see in my country and elsewhere in the world, East and West, such as unemployment, poverty, oppression, corruption, religious exploitation, and sexual harassment. We live in one world, not three. It is governed by one international power – military, capitalist, racist and religious – that uses known and hidden methods to control nations. The Arab nations being torn apart by recent wars are a case in point. Israel, which sits close to the top of international powers, dreams of annihilating the Arab world, and has in fact attained some of that dream, thanks to our national Arab governments and their US government friends.

The Economist (4 May 2017) published an article titled 'The Sorry State of Arab Men', based on research conducted in four Arab countries – Egypt, Palestine, Lebanon,

Morocco – which finds that Arab men suffer from a 'crisis of masculinity' because of the increase in poverty and their inability to provide, and that this makes them more violent and more likely to sexually harass women. This type of research abounds in academia and serves to disguise attempts to misrepresent certain nations or ideologies, for the benefit of certain political powers. Politics governs science and research like it does media and religion and education and moral values. There is no such thing as 'objectivity' in this cruel world built on deception and violence.

Ahram Weekly published my response to that article, under the title 'The Sorry State of the World' (18 May 2017), after *The Economist* refused to publish it (further evidence of the false claim of objectivity). I pointed out how the research addresses the violence of Palestinian men in isolation from the violence of the Israeli-American occupation of their lands and homes, and with no comparison with Israeli or American men, thus pretending that sexual violence is somehow linked to Arab genes, instead of the outcome of the actions of a global, class-based patriarchal military, as well as educational and religious orders, which go as far back in history as the moment Eve was found culpable and Adam was absolved of sin.

Patriarchal violence is closely linked to economic violence in the framework of both world powers and religious terrorist organisations, like Daesh, Boko Haram and others. *The Economist*'s article goes on to portray the crime of female genital mutilation as an Arab identity practice, ignoring the fact that it is not practised in most Arab countries (including Saudi Arabia).

Equality in Oppression

The new Press Regulation law reminds me of the Indecency Law that put me and others in prison in September 1981. Words like 'disturbance' and 'disrespect' which are mentioned in the new law evoke the idea of what is 'inappropriate' and what is considered beneficial to family values and village traditions. That is, the same principles that put us in prison over fourteen years ago until a regime change let us go with no criminal charges. We spent three months in prison, then we were released without receiving compensation, financial or moral, for the injustice we had endured.

That measure of temporary detainment is still unjustly used and defended by officials and members of the parliament to this day under the false pretence of equality and law. As if equal distribution of injustice is how fairness is defined. Injustice should be eradicated not normalised.

Apparently, someone discovered Clause 40 in the constitution which states that all citizens are equal before the law. They then deduced that arbitrary and temporary detainment should be applied to everyone, not discriminating between those who carry pens and those who carry knives.

Naturally I support the constitution, especially the clause that declares equality between citizens regardless of ethnicity, class, religion, etc. What I would call for is for that non-discriminatory treatment to be truly applied to everyone, not just those who write for the press.

In theory, increased authority should come with increased responsibility, accountability and punishment for mistakes or lies told to the people. The press is but the fourth of the third known power, the other three being: the legislative, the executive, and the judicial. The measure of preventive detention should be brought to bear on members of those three powers before it begins to affect writers and journalists.

In theory also, all Egyptian laws should be revised because they contradict Clause 40 which proposes all citizens to be equal. But do marriage and divorce laws treat all citizens equally regardless of gender?

Why don't the members of the parliament defend constitutional equality in all cases for all citizens, not just when it comes to a specific group. In theory, the law is meant to protect the people against those in power, and not the other way around. The more power a person has, the less immunity and impunity they should be granted, and not the other way around.

What such upside-down principles tell us is that justice in our country is not just blindfolded but blind, and that it is power that decides what laws are upheld or revised.

The question of the press is making headlines at the moment because, after all, the press has a voice and is capable of using it to defend itself. But our country is full of groups suffering injustices – women, wives, mothers, and children, whether under family law, nationality law, or criminal law – and these groups remain without a voice or power on this battlefield where power always wins over justice.

Political Islam

Political Islam, as a term, has gained prevalence since the dual presidencies of Ronald Reagan in the US and Anwar Sadat in Egypt, in the 1970s. Their politics resulted in strengthening and emboldening the religion-based political and terrorist movements, including Islamist groups like al-Qaeda, Taleban, Daesh (ISIS), Boko Haram, the Muslim Brotherhood, Hamas and so on.

We must study the history of each political religion-based faction – be it Islamic, Jewish, Christian or other – in order to find out how it originated, and what were the national and international powers that supported it financially or militarily.

Let's take for instance how French colonialists planned to conquer Egypt in 1798. The Leibniz Egypt Plan (developed by the German philosopher a century earlier) emphasised the importance of religion, as a weapon equal to military ones, in conquering nations. That lesson, which Leibniz garnered from Europe's Christian wars during medieval times was also reflected in the actions of Napoleon Bonaparte. When he set out to conquer Egypt through military and economic means, he allegedly proclaimed to the Egyptian people that the French were loyal Muslims too. He all but converted to Islam to perfect his deception.

British colonialism too was adept at using religion to deceive colonised nations. The words spoken by an African peasant summed it up. She said, 'The English gave us the Bible and took the land.' British colonialism collaborated with Egyptian monarchs to strengthen the Muslim Brotherhood since their establishment in the 1920s. The aim was to counter the anti-capitalist socialist and communist popular movements, and to divide Egypt by creating and stoking a sectarian conflict between Muslims and Copts.

Israel learned the same lesson from the British and emboldened the Islamist Hamas to weaken the popular movements of the Palestinian resistance, including the PLO under Yasser Arafat's leadership.

American neo-colonialism too inherited the expertise of British colonialism of old and used Islam as a tool in military and political conflict and to ignite sectarian conflict across the Arab world.

For as long as it existed in the world and throughout history, religion has been used in politics.

If we study the history of Judaism, Christianity, Islam or any other religion, we would realise that these were political economic movements from the start. The earthly ruler would gain power over his people by wearing the cloak of divinity. Clergymen and priests played a role in keeping the people ignorant, with religious teachings and blind faith enforced from childhood.

If we study the three holy books – the Old Testament, the Bible, and the Qur'an – we see that they are political books hiding under the cover of God's word. People's minds fail to see through the deception because of the teachings imposed on them from childhood. A mature mind might rationally uncover the truth, but religious faith continues to burden the conscience, or what is referred to as the soul.

The occupation of Palestinian land with military force is a political, economic, and military action that uses religious claims to justify itself.

Practices like hijab and niqab and patrilineality are economic and political sexual practices. They use religious claims to justify themselves.

My father, who spent his life studying theology in a number of institutions, didn't just study Islam and its history, but also the history of other Abrahamic religions, as well as some non-Abrahamic religions like Buddhism and Hinduism. He read works by philosophers and poets – Ibn Sina, al-Jahiz, Ibn Rushd, al-Mutanabbi, Abu Nuwas, Bashar ibn Burd, Abu al-Alaa al-Maarri, Rabindranath Tagore, Khalil Gibran, Taha Hussein. Listening to him speak used to fill me with joy. His words filled me with a kind of human dignity that was so unlike what I felt when I listened to religion teachers and preachers in mosques and on the radio. When the latter talked about women, my heart sank and humiliation engulfed me.

My father would say the essence of all religions is the same, in line with reason, with justice, health, freedom and happiness, with creativity and beauty and love and dignity, for men and women alike. But teachers and government clerks at religious institutions in all countries, preachers and rabbis and priests and sheikhs and holy

men, they are all preoccupied with serving the powers that
be. They ignore the essential values of religion – justice,
equality, dignity and freedom – and focus on rites and
clothing and beards, ordinations and liturgies and altars.
That's why the world is drowning in wars that are simulta-
neously political and religious. Battles rage between sects
and ideologies and unchallenged holy texts, which all
discriminate between human beings on grounds of race,
gender, class, and sect.

My mother and father raised me on the love of books,
discovery, travel, and researching history, science and the
arts. In the 1970s, I lived in India and met writers like
Kamala Das and Amrita Pritam. I met Indira Gandhi and
engaged in debates with her. I lay down on a bed of nails
and spent a few full-moon nights in Gandhi's ashram.
An Indian philosopher I met at the ashram told me how
Gandhi did not separate religion and politics. She also said
that if God wanted Indians to believe in him, he should
send them bread.

I stayed home for a few days in New Delhi reading the
Gita, the Hindu scripture that inspired many psychology experts and political scientists in the modern world.
Still, any religious philosophy, no matter how progressive,
cannot keep up with scientific progress. To this day, religion remains a weapon serving racist, patriarchal, and
classist wars.

Between Two Seas

Today I write from Barcelona where Catalans display their history, arts, and deep-rooted civilisation. I've been here before, fourteen years ago, as a visiting professor at the Universitat Autònoma (the Autonomous University of Barcelona), a university that goes against the grain of stale academic moulds and traditions. I taught my favourite subject, 'Women's Creativity and Rebellion'. My books were translated into Spanish and Catalan and taught at the university. I was awarded the Premi Internacional Catalunya, which they hold in as high a regard as the Swedes hold the Nobel Prize. They have an international event where the president of Catalonia speaks. When I heard him say, 'Behind every great woman stands a great man,' I stood up and said, 'This might be true for men who need great women behind them but not for women!' The large audience that filled the hall burst out laughing. I wondered if the president considered withholding my award then.

Yesterday, after I gave a talk for International Women's Day, a tall and slender woman came towards me and warmly shook my hand. She said, 'I used to be a student in your class at university. Today I'm a writer and poet, and I have come to thank you.' I answered, 'It's me who should thank you, because this is my true reward.'

The sun shone and the sea glistened under the golden

sun. The statue of Columbus stood erect where it has always stood, pointing to the south, towards Egypt and Africa, and not towards America. I saw him from my window every morning as I drank my coffee and prepared myself to work on my new novel, which was later published in Egypt by Dar al-Hilal under the title *The Novel*. It told the story of a young woman who migrates from Cairo to Barcelona and wanders in its streets like in a museum. There is a historically and artistically valuable building on every street. Then there is the Sagrada Família, the world's largest cathedral. The Catalan tour guide was full of pride when she said, 'The design of this cathedral materialised in Gaudí's mind at the start of the twentieth century, and the construction carried on after his death until this day. It's scheduled to finish in nine years, once the Paradise Tower is completed.'

'Can I enter the Paradise Tower,' I asked her with childish excitement. 'Paradise is under construction. Also, Dr Saadawi,' she laughed, 'Women have no place in paradise. Isn't that what you named one of your stories? I read it in Catalan translation eleven years ago.' I was surprised by her response. 'Eleven years ago?!' I exclaimed in my Egyptian Arabic which she understood a bit of. 'Yes, eleven years ago.'

We carried on. 'All towers, except for the Paradise Tower, are open to visitors. Antonio Gaudí believed that Christ died on the cross, was buried and resurrected. He designed these eighteen towers to embody the different stages in the life of Christ, starting with his birth and his life with his mother the Virgin Mary and his earthly father, Joseph the carpenter. His heavenly father protected him during the sacred family's journey to Egypt, the land of the Nile. This door is one of seven large bronze doors and it carries in Catalan the words that Christ said in his prayers. There is the phrase "Lord give us our daily bread" engraved in fifty languages including Arabic. There are engravings in the bronze of the flowers of the Nile and its plants and animals. Look at this *tortuga* swimming in the Nile.'

At 86, I wasn't going to climb up any of the towers. But I was invited to speak at another international conference, somewhere on the coast of the Mediterranean near the Catalan-French border. I appeared in the conference in conversation with Lluís Bassets, editor-in-chief of *El País*, the second-most circulated daily newspaper in Spain. I challenged some of his perceptions about women in the Arab and Muslim worlds, and the audience stood up and clapped in agreement with me. One of the professors at the Universitat Autònoma said, 'The Catalan people are protesting against the racist policies of European govern-ments. We welcome migrants!'

The conference administration gave me a few histori-cal books about Palafrugell on Costa Brava. Among its distinctive features are the sculptures made from tree barks, and Cap Roig, the red-brick citadel surrounded by botanical gardens on a hill overlooking the sea, the most beautiful place on earth – maybe that's where paradise was. I lay on the beach under a warm, gentle sun and let

my imagination stretch itself from Sharm el-Sheikh on the
Red Sea to the coast of Catalonia on the Mediterranean,
from a place that would erase my existence to a place that
honours me and celebrates my words.

When Does the Fall Begin?

Despite the upheavals of war and peace, Beirut remains standing strong, like the goddess Inanna or Ishtar, her high mountains and deep sea soak up the poison and turn it under the sun into oxygen that dissolves in the warm blood of its people's veins, recreating Beirut in ever renewable brilliance.

I first knew war and violence through my Lebanese doctor friend during the late seventies and early eighties. Until she was stabbed by an Israeli soldier at Sabra and Shatila where she was treating the injured and died on her feet like a tree. I was working for the UN at the time, at ECWA which later changed to ESCWA – nothing changes but the names while the piles of reports remain the same. I used to open my window for some fresh air and hear the ringing sound of bullets coming from the sea and the mountain.

Who was at war with whom? Nobody knew. Israelis, Americans, Palestinians, Lebanese, Muslims, Shia, Sunni, Christians of fifteen different sects. While in the UN's chic corridors experts of all colours strutted up and down, all puffed up, reeking of Eau Sauvage and dangling pipes between their lips while they exchanged news and told jokes, as if there was no war, no blood flowing in the streets and refugee camps. They winked at the heavily made-up secretaries with their eyebrows-plucked, organised South conferences in the winter and North conferences in the summer, and returned to Beirut to eat kofta and tabbouleh and drink arak.

The city of conferences, conspiracies, and publishers, where everything is bought and sold, where writers' rights is won and lost, the city of conversations and contradictions, where missiles explode by day and dancefloors erupt with music by night. In Beirut, virtue and sin go hand in hand, nudity and hijab, love and war.

In April this year, I gave a talk at a university conference in Beirut. I did not separate violence against women from other kinds of violence, or national from international violence, or sexual violence from economic, political, and religious violence.

Violence against women is a historical and global occurrence – it is not a phenomenon specific to either the East or the West. I have been repeating this for more than half a century. But we still separate gender violence from other subjects in academia, lest we expose the close historical links between gendered slavery and class slavery, and the martial, colonialist orders they generated.

A question asked at the conference was, 'What is the link between global women's protests and President Trump', to which an American NYU professor responded, 'It's impossible for women to liberate themselves under a standard capitalist system, let alone a vicious one like Tump's.'

And she was right. It was only a few days later when

Trump revealed his patriarchal militant tendencies and
bombed the Syrians. Fifty-nine Tomahawk missiles,
launched out of two Navy cruisers, destroyed the Shayrat
Airbase near Homs. This constituted a glaring breach of
the UN Charter and international treaties and the rules
of law and ethics. It was no different from the actions of
George W Bush, when he destroyed Baghdad with missiles, under the pretence of saving the Iraqi people from
the dictator Saddam and his alleged weapons of mass
destruction. Only the names have changed. Trump bombs
Syria under the pretence of saving the Syrian people from
the dictator Bashar al-Assad and his weapons of chemical
warfare.

The UN only has one response: urging self-control
and asking all parties to return to the negotiation table.
Nothing ever changes, since the beginning of the Israeli
occupation of Palestine and to this day. The negotiation
table, of course, means more feasts for the experts and
consultants, the chef's choice with the best wines, on the
Swiss hills in summer and under the Indian sun in winter.

The human jungle is populated with tigers and hyenas
urging self-control and expecting everyone to hold their
breaths while they puff away on their pipes.

When I returned from Beirut, I found Egyptians in a
state of anxious anticipation: What was the government
going to do to control the market and tackle the rise in
prices during the imminent month of Ramadan? And how
does that month of fasting and renunciation turn into a
month of gluttony and greed? How could trade thrive on

fatwas and TV series and belly dances? Women's rights organisations announced seminars to confront the issue of sexual harassment during Ramadan.

With Knowledge Comes Pleasure

It's the month of May and the world is blossoming. A person's mind starts to open like a flower, and we eat honey, the result of the bee's adoration of the flower. Although I can no longer afford a good jar of honey. My friend has honey-coloured eyes. When she looks at the moon, her heart beats with love, not for anyone in particular, but for all living beings, even stones. She holds a piece of rock in her hands and observes it with childish wonder.

'Why are you so impressed with this stone?'

'Why aren't you?'

'There's nothing impressive about it.'

'Old age begins where wonder ends.'

'Did you have honey and almonds for breakfast?'

'I feel the rock pulsing in my hand.'

'How can I feel the pulse of a rock on an empty stomach?'

'You are a prisoner of reality, my friend.'

Nothing reveals truth like the imagination. We cannot gain knowledge without imagining and inventing. How can we rescue knowledge from the claws of hunger and oppression and nuclear and thermobaric bombs? When are we going to recognise knowledge as real virtue, instead of women's head veils and increased religion lessons in school?

Is it possible to be liberated from twenty-first-century

slavery when poverty is on the rise? In the United States, 1% of the population own everything, while the rest are struggling; never mind what goes on in poor countries like ours.

When children look at the moon and wonder where it came from, parents and teachers have no answers. They didn't study the origins of the moon and the earth and the sun and the stars. They know little about the primary matter of the universe, about atoms and electrons. They work on computers all day and don't understand how they work.

Why do lovers gaze at the moon? How does the moon influence the tidal movements of the sea, or the circulatory system of blood in our bodies?

Why did the church condemn the first scientists who discovered the earth was round and moved in an orbit? What is it about scientific exploration that scares men of God? And what's the link between knowledge expansion and the evolution of the brain, of imagination and creativity?

My friend was telling me about the link between the moon and the piece of rock, while I was preoccupied with the rise in the prices of honey and Ramadan treats.

She taught me a lesson when she said, 'If you don't know the moon's origins, you live in darkness.' She proceeded to explain how scientists never ceased their explorations into the origins of the moon. They admitted the error of earlier theories which said that the earth's rapid rotation around its axis resulted in a piece of it breaking off and that became the basis of the moon. That is, the theory that the moon is the offspring of the earth. But material analysis proved that the making of the earth's rock is different from the moon's. The search for answers continued, with researchers eventually proposing that the moon was not part of our solar system, and that it was caught by the earth's gravity and pulled into its orbit. Later scientists discovered that the moon was formed in the same way as the earth, i.e. from cosmic debris and interstellar dust that accumulated to form the earth, the moon, and the planets. The latest hypothesis though, developed in the nineties, says that the moon may have been formed from the collision of the earth with another planet and parts breaking off from both of them to form the moon. The collision is supposed to have been tangential. Scientists still continue to research and to develop their findings to arrive at a relatively correct hypothesis. For there are no final truths in science, only ever-evolving research and experiments, giving us electricity, airplanes, computers, and endless future possibilities.

But isn't it the same scientific knowledge that produced weapons of mass destruction? This is probably a product of the power governments exercise over scientists and the means of channelling knowledge towards arms manufacture and military invasions. How do they achieve this? By bribing scientists and intellectuals with money and awards and prestige. Those who reject the bribe are killed, exiled, imprisoned, or defamed in the media.

And why don't nations defend their innovators?

Because they are kept in ignorance by education systems that threaten free thinking and creativity with punishment in this life and the next. Freethinkers go to prison on charges of blasphemy, and whole populations stop wondering about the world and become preoccupied instead with the prices of honey and Ramadan treats.

Does the pleasure of gazing at the moon diminish with the knowledge that it is a dark rock? On the contrary, we understand then that it is a living entity and this knowledge increases the pleasure.

The Price of Writing

I'm no good at writing introductions. I could write a story
a thousand pages long, but falter at a half-page introduc-
tion. But my lifelong friend is a mysterious creature. She
writes whether she's asleep or awake, ignoring the planet's cycles or its movement around the sun. She would
laugh and say, 'We are free to orbit whatever we want,
ourselves, another person, or stay in one place. But my
mind goes round and round against my will, in my sleep
or wakefulness.'

I wake up every morning to the sound of the phone
ringing, her voice coming to me from whichever corner of
the planet she happens to be. She has loved travelling since
childhood. She would barely come home before she was
off again. But however long she stays away, I always see
her outside my door, with her old wine-coloured suitcase
that has been scorched by the southern sun and soaked
by the northern rain. It has become a bit less red than it
used to be, though hasn't completely lost its colour, still
has maintained its robust wheels and some of the strength
of its body. She pulls it behind her across airports and
train stations, and the suitcase gracefully obliges, sliding
over smoothly paved streets and sinking its weight onto
the surface of cobbled or bumpy alleyways, filled with her
books and clothes and papers, sporting a sturdy handle

to which a rectangular plastic label the size of her hand is attached, carrying her name.

Her full three-part name is registered in the records of the ministries of Interior and Social Affairs, the Central Prison Administration, and the various departments responsible for the control and censorship of publications and artistic works.

The passport control police officer at Cairo Airport stares at her full name and examines her photograph before smiling at her. 'Welcome back, Professor!' He stamps her passport and asks her to follow him. The blacklist must have landed before she did. He apologises with a gentleness he must have inherited from his mother, offers her a chair and a glass of water. 'I'm sorry, Professor. There are instructions that I must follow.' If the officer happens to be a follower of an Islamist group or the ruling party, however, he would bare his teeth and mutter under his breath, before leading her with her red suitcase to a detention room, where she would meet all kinds of individuals. Some would have been placed in quarantine with diseases that range from leprosy to swine flu, others are either mad and or are disbelievers.

Once there was a hairdresser, Sousou, who enjoyed a degree of fame in the posh neighbourhood of Zamalek. He gained a rare kind of education from the time he spent cutting men's and women's hair. His deft fingers recognised the quality of thoughts inside the heads they touched. The neighbourhood residents came to his chic

salon on the Street of Sighs, men and women of the edu-
cated upper classes, those who believed that humans have
evolved from the same ancestors as the great mother, the
chimpanzee, and that the earth is round and orbits the
sun and not the other way around, and that the universe
started as a cosmic accident when the big bang scattered
subatomic particles in space that later coalesced as atoms
to form the first matter.

Among Sousou's clients were also the concierges and
cooks in the palaces of old and new pashas in Zamalek and
Garden City. Among those was Hajj Mansour, the pasha's
cook, a large man whose figure showed the saturated and
sumptuous food he received more than his share of in the
pasha's kitchen. And while his coif was safely managed by
Sousou's hands, he told stories about the Mamluks and the
Turks, and life in Anatolia. He always listed his ancestors
starting with this great-grandfather who in his childhood
had told him that God created the bull with two horns so
he could carry the earth on one horn, and if he got tired,
move it to the other horn.

'That's so funny, Hajj Mansour!' Sousou laughed.

'But it's true, Sousou,' Hajj Mansour said. 'Where do
you think earthquakes and volcanoes and thunder and
lightning come from?'

'Where do they come from, Hajj Mansour?'

'When the bull moves the earth from one horn to the
other, the shift shakes the earth.'

Sousou laughed, 'That's so funny, Hajj Mansour.'

'It's true, Sousou.'

'That must have been before the time of Galileo.'

'Galileo was a foreigner and an infidel, Sousou. He knew no God.'

'Look, Hajj,' Sousou said, 'I must tell you about Galileo.'

'I'm listening, brother.'

'Galileo was born in Italy one-thousand and five-hundred years or more after Virgin Mary gave birth to Christ. Italy and Europe were all under the rule of the church, living in ignorance and darkness. Galileo studied medicine and engineering and astronomy. He began to discover the errors of philosophers before him in Greece, including Aristotle.'

'Did Aristotle believe in God, Sousou?'

'Aristotle believed in religion, Hajj Mansour. He spread religious ideas in his books, so the religious institution considered him the greatest philosopher, and heaped money and honours upon him. But Galileo built a new telescope and proved Aristotle wrong. He said that the earth rotates on its access and around the sun. So the church got angry at him and accused him of blasphemy and treason, because he contradicted the holy book, the church's teachings, and Aristotle's theory about the earth being motionless and fixed for eternity. They prosecuted and condemned him and he died poor and isolated in his home.'

'Who told you all this?'

'The pasha when I was trimming his beard and moustache.'

'The pasha himself, Sousou?'

'Yes, Hajj Mansour.'

'It must be true then,' Hajj Mansour said. 'But I don't feel that the earth is rotating, Sousou.'

'That's because it's very fast, Hajj. And you're part of it and move with it.'

'That doesn't make sense, Sousou.'

'It's the same as when you're riding a train, Hajj,' Sousou persisted. 'You don't feel it move because you're in it and it's moving very fast.'

'But a train is one thing and the earth is another, Sousou. No?'

'No, Hajj!'

Both Sousou and Hajj Mansour burst out laughing.

She, my lifelong friend, would leave the quarantine room pulling her red suitcase on its wheels after a few hours or a few days, depending on what the government and the secret intelligence service fancied. Her dress would be wrinkled and her hair dishevelled. She would have slept in a chair with her suitcase beside her, close enough for her hand to touch if she suddenly woke up in the dark. She worried someone would steal it while she was fast asleep, passed out from exhaustion. Then one morning, without warning, the smiling officer comes and says, 'Congratulations, Professor! There's been a presidential pardon because of the holidays.'

'What holiday?'

It would be Eid al-Adha, or the Great Crossing of the Suez Canal, or Sham Ennessim at the start of spring. If it's the latter, people would be waking up early to breathe in the smell of onion and herring and salted fish, then go for walks along the Nile. The rich amongst them would take their fresh air in the new resorts on the Mediterranean coast or the Red Sea. Salted fish from Nabaroh remains the best, served with a variety of delicious dishes, spring onions and herring, all necessary to make the holiday complete and revive childhood memories and ancestral history.

I've always loved salted fish, while she can't stand its smell. She never visits me when it's in season. She generally doesn't celebrate holidays, doesn't even remember her own birthday. If I mention it, she would just twist her lower lip and busy herself with writing.

'How old are you?'

'I don't remember.'

'You're unbelievable.'

'So are you.'

'Why?'

'What do you care about my age.'

'I want to know how many years you've lived.'

'Why?'

'I don't know.'

An Old Friend

I came across an Arabic newspaper, here on this faraway small island in the north of the Atlantic Ocean, where all I see is the line where the sea meets the sky, and the fish racing underwater, caught here and there in the beaks of white seagulls that soar like eagles, or like tiny jet planes, and swoop down upon the small fish that swim merrily away from their parents. Small fish are always the ones who get eaten, whether in the water, on land, or up in heaven. The old God destroys lives and livelihoods with earthquakes and volcanoes, and incites his followers to kill others and steal their land, their olive trees and their food.

All for what? The same question preoccupied me over half a century ago. Back then you told me that my rational mind is incapable of understanding divine wisdom. We disagreed about the definitions of rationality, wisdom, and balance. My questions used to make you angry because they challenged the beliefs you inherited from your father and grandfather. I would accuse you of rigidity, and you would accuse me of insanity, and we would part ways for a while. But we always returned. Something connected us that was bigger than rationality and divine wisdom – we didn't quite know what it was and we didn't try to find out. Life distracted us with its small and large calamities:

your child has diarrhoea, my child has a cold, there's been a new attack on Palestine, on Iraq, Syria, Lebanon, Korea, Somalia, Iran, or Libya. Oh how many wars we have witnessed, how many peace treaties, how many natural and manmade disasters, how many thousands or millions have we seen killed by earthquakes or volcanoes or burned by napalm or bombs that break through steel.

So I happened to read the newspaper and in it was your obituary. The muscle in my heart that I felt contract then has no name in medical science. It's made of more than flesh and muscle tissue, of other material perhaps, psychological and cerebral, social and historical, and spiritual. We didn't cover the soul in medical school. The mysterious soul falls under spirituality and belongs in religious studies. I used to laugh and say that we have a spiritual bond, pure and poisonous, nothing physical in it, not defiled by sex. Your green eyes would sparkle with something black and wolf-like as you reluctantly agreed with me.

The Arabic newspaper carrying your obituary was delivered to me by the man who lives in the house with the ocean view next to mine. His name is Bill. He lives alone and writes poetry and carves sculptures that fill his garden. His primary hobby though is to sail in his small boat with the white sail that makes me think of the Nile. He has a special dock at the end of his front garden. In the back garden, he has a wire-fenced area where he grows tomatoes, spinach, lettuce, and garden rocket which is called arugula in American English – that is, twisted

English, if you're British, and refined English, if you're American. I ask about rocket leaves everywhere I travel, and when I first visited London, forty years ago, no one knew what it was. What is it about this particular leaf that makes me seek it wherever I go? It may be a spiritual bond that connects me to that delicate, pungent, powerfully green plant. I'd definitely categorise its fragrance under 'spiritual' – the moment the scent floods my lungs, I feel my soul awaken. I remember my mother's face when I was a child, as she cut the leaves and arranged them on the plate, with me watching her with wide unblinking eyes, the fragrance of rocket spreading all over my body and permeating my senses with the sun's warmth and my mother's presence.

Here in the north of the north, I sit in my room over-looking the vast ocean and watch the rain turn into snow-flakes. The temperature is below zero, the trees have shed their leaves in red and orange and brown and yellow, and because red stands out, the ground under my feet as I take my morning walk looks like it's covered by a crimson carpet. The leaves tremble under my thick rubber shoes, as if they still have life in them. I watch the horizon of white clouds and I am filled with longing, for my mother, the sun at home, and my little sister.

Perhaps in your death, my friend, you no longer care about the sun making an appearance at the end of autumn in a far nameless island. But here, radio descriptions of every detail of daily weather – sunny, windy, various tem-peratures – don't stop. People here are more concerned with the temperature dropping or rising by two or three degrees than they ever will be with the murder of three-thousand souls who used to live somewhere beyond the sea.

The newspaper came to me inside a basket filled with garden rocket and violets that Bill had brought me. He is in his seventies, tall and slender, his blue eyes sparkle in the sun and, like the sky and ocean water, change in autumn to a smoky grey and sometimes mercurial silver. His gaze remains strong and piercing, as if an ageless spirit looks out of his eyes, one that knows no old age and no death. He doesn't read Arabic, but he picks up Arabic newspapers for me on his boat trips south to Boston or New York City to take part in anti-war or anti-globalisation protests. He reads the *New York Times* every day and calls it Zionist and reactionary. He says the paper supported Bush and Sharon, despite publishing the occasional good article from the opposition just to maintain a democratic baseline. Despite being over seventy years old, Bill runs around the island for five miles every morning. The skin on his face is as taut as his muscles, he could be a young man in his thirties or forties. I started to run around the island too, beginning at my house at the end of Point Road – called that because it ends at the sea, the end point of the island. I chose this house because I can see the ocean from my bedroom windows while writing my new novel. Since childhood I've loved the idea of writing while sitting in a bed with an open window overlooking an open horizon.

I read your obituary, my friend, when I turned to the

obituary pages at the back of the newspaper. I never used to read those pages when I was younger. My father used to read them regularly, and I used to wonder at his interest in the dead. Until he died and I started copying some of his habits instead of rebelling against them, possibly out of a guilty conscience or because I missed my absent father, or for some other mysterious historical and psychological reason. Obituary pages now haunt me like the spectre of love.

I was browsing when my eyes spotted your name, written in a large font at the top of a long obituary that covered five or six columns. A black rectangle framed a photo of you holding your pointed chin between your thumb and index finger like a Greek philosopher. There was also a photo from your funeral, line after line of important looking men, surrounding their president who stood in the middle of the front line in black sunglasses and a black tie. You couldn't have seen all these important men, standing there with exaggerated sadness behind their dark glasses. Some must have been hiding the kind of glee people sometimes feel at funerals just for knowing they're not the ones who died, especially if the dead person was more distinguished even in death, their coffin wrapped in the national flag like yours was. Such glory, my friend, must have been envied by some of your fellow writers and intellectuals.

I didn't expect to read your obituary from this faraway island in the middle of the ocean. It had been two years since I last saw you, but you were full of energy then. You were on your way to get into your black Mercedes, outside your house on Giza Street, your neat-looking driver having started the engine, when you spotted me and stopped. 'Nawal?' you called to me. 'Unbelievable! It's been so long! Your hair is white as snow, but it's charming. You haven't changed in thirty years.'

'Well, Mohamed, maybe I'm just stuck.'

'No Nawal! You have a kind of eternal youth, that's what it is!'

'You haven't changed either, Mohamed.'

'Oh no, I'm an old man now.'

We carried on talking like we used to thirty years ago. Your driver came to remind you of your important meeting – maybe with the president or prime minister – but you paid no attention to him. You gestured towards your front door, inviting me in for a cup of coffee. I followed you into the large garden, and from there to the porch and entrance, then to the reception room with its elegant green velvet reception furniture. You stopped before an elegant display case, reminiscent of the cupboards where the rich store their silverware. I had seen one of those in my grandfather's house when I was six. You pointed to the awards arranged inside the case, in gold and silver and bronze, with your name engraved next to the date of when you had received each award: the National Merit and National Incentive Awards, Literary Excellence Award, awards from Nasser, Sadat and Mubarak, awards from China, Japan, Korea, Iran, Iraq, even Palestine. As well as an award from the Palestinian revolution movement, there were awards from several popular resistance movements in African, Asian and South American countries. I found it hard to follow what you were telling me about the history of each award. There was also an Arabesque bookcase holding your publications, fiction and non-fiction, all with gold-illuminated covers carrying your name and your father's and grandfather's names. I saw that wolfish sparkle in your eyes again. I knew you wanted to impress me, to demonstrate proof of your genius. I remember this look from when we first met at the Story Club on Qasr El Eyni Street. I was a young woman then, but I had the ability to see what other girls my age didn't. And I hated that look in your eyes. The look that said that you were cleverer than me, and that I would have no choice but to fall for you. But the opposite happened, and it was you who fell for me, my friend. I fell in love with another man.

The last time I saw you was perhaps at a literary conference at the Cairo Book Fair, where awards were being bestowed on those considered to be great thinkers by the regime. You were one of them. I saw you trot confidently to the stage, your head held high, proud in an elegant dark suit and red tie (maybe a last nod towards your allegiance with the left). You held your posture erect, but when you were two steps away from the president, you bowed so deeply I thought you had a sudden pancreatic attack or something. But you were soon standing tall again – perhaps roused by your conscience. You left the stage with the award hanging next to you like a disabled limb, and as soon as you took your seat, you met my eyes and hid the award between your legs, like a secret mistress giving you secret pleasure.

Even when I was still about thirty-two, you found it strange that I didn't read the obituaries. You, my friend, thought this was the most important section in the news-paper, since it discloses hidden alliances, various ties of kinship, social networks and influence hubs. I remember your words after more than forty years. Your eyes were as green as grass. But you saw the black of my eyes as more beautiful than all the green and blue eyes in the world. Maybe that's why I didn't forget your words with the passage of time. I started reading the obituary pages and haven't stopped since. Maybe they became linked to an important fact in my life, which is that my eyes are the most beautiful in the world.

'You know, Nawal, the obituary pages are extremely important.'

'Why, Mohamed?'

And you would speak at length about the benefits of those pages. You would explain how they were like genes and chromosomes, revealing degrees of kinship and separation. 'What is carried in the lines of the obituary pages, Nawal,' you would say, 'and between the lines, are glimpses of clandestine relationships, stories of love and hate, peeked at from behind closed doors, the little secrets concealed under the collection of truths and lies that make up our real lives.'

I started reading the obituary pages and the accident and crime reports too, which you also praised. You said these were more important than the front pages which hold nothing but the photographs of presidents and kings, war developments and peace treaties.

As I held the newspaper with news of your death in my hands, I remembered a small news story I had seen online a while ago about your granddaughter Nuriya, the daughter of your eldest son. She who carries your name and the names of your son and your father and grandfather. Your granddaughter was suddenly gone from your big Garden City house with the Nile view. Nineteen-year-old Nuriya disappeared and didn't leave a note for her parents, or for her award-winning renowned intellectual grandfather, who is praised by everyone for his patriotism, his knowledge, his faith, his uprightness. How could the straight rib of such a man produce a crooked offspring? But Nuriya used to be a model girl, she did well in school and was engaged to a model young man from a good family. The fiancé had an excellent educational record, good manners, and never missed a patriotic event or a poetry reading. Her father and grandfather were proud of that brilliant young man. Both families had been making arrangements for a big wedding at the Meridian Hotel. Over a thousand invitations had already been printed, on engraved paper with gold-illuminated corners.

I read the news online while I was living on the island at the other end of the world, and imagined myself as that runaway granddaughter. At her age, I too thought about running away. What occupied my mind in the year 1951 when I was nineteen years old? When I thought about leaving, my friend, and didn't know where to go? What were the things that mattered to me more than family and home and love and a future husband? That question did not seem to have crossed anyone's mind in your respectable family. All you could imagine was that the girl must have fallen in love and was pregnant by a man other than her legitimate fiancé.

I wasn't in love with any man when I was nineteen. I had fallen in love a few times from the time I was ten, and by then I had reached the conclusion that I was made for a bigger role than love and marriage and motherhood and so on, and that I would never be like my mother and grandmother and sister. No man would ever own me, even if he was the king of the world.

A girl like the one I'd been is usually diagnosed by psychiatrists as a case who needs to be held in hospital and cured with chemicals or electric shocks, or maybe a lobotomy to get rid of that part of the brain where strong emotions and wild imagination reside.

I believe that the news about your granddaughter's disappearance came a few days before your death. Maybe it was the shock that hastened your end. How could your granddaughter leave your grand house, abandon your name and the names of your father and grandfather, take off the silver necklace that carries your picture and the gold watch you gave her when she scored 99.9% in her high school exams, which is a grade that only just falls short of absolute perfection, because only God is meant to reach a full 100%. It must have been absolute 100% evil, the devil or Iblis, who is cursed in this life and the next, who whispered in your granddaughter's ear and made her reject the riches of her family and the honours bestowed on her paternal ancestors. Who else but the Devil himself could make a nineteen-year-old girl reject the age-old inherited traditions – family, homeland and national flag, religious faith, love, marriage and motherhood?

I don't know where your granddaughter could have run to, my friend. I know that in 1951, when I was her age, I didn't know where to go. The radio played songs declaring eternal love for the king on a daily basis. Newspapers and magazines called him the virtuous king. Distinguished writers and intellectuals like yourself, my friend, praised him in essays and poems and keynote speeches. Al-Azhar sheikhs prayed in public mosques that he shall live and rule long. The king sat in the front row at concerts and other events, the national anthem played for him and singers like Mohammed Abdel Wahab and Umm Kulthum blessed his name.

I was nineteen, the same age as your runaway granddaughter, and I used to bite my fingernails until they tore out of anger and frustration. It didn't take much intelligence to realise that this was a corrupt world singing for a corrupt king. But I couldn't utter the words 'corrupt king' when the whole world around me called him virtuous. There was a bridge called The Virtuous King (Al-Malek al-Saleh), and a large square named King Farouk Square, as well as a major street and the main university in Giza. Not to mention public libraries, research centres, train stations, and boys' schools all carried the king's name. Girls' schools, on the other hand, were normally named after the king's wife. Now they carry the name of 'the first lady', as Americans say.

I was the same age as your granddaughter, looking around me in disbelief. Was the world mad, or was I? At nineteen, I had great confidence in myself and in my intellect. But how could one sane person remain sane when surrounded by insanity?

I too was driven out of my mind, my friend, and I did exactly what your granddaughter did. I discarded the picture of my respectable grandfather, discarded the names of my father and his fathers, and threw off my neck the silver necklace that carried a gold heart-shaped pendant with three words: God, Country, King. The three words we chanted at school every morning. I discarded too the silky white angelic wedding dress, and put on my grey gabardine overcoat and white trainers. In my pocket I had twenty-three pence that I imagined were enough for a ticket to another non-corrupt world.

That was on 12 November 1951. My respectable family was making wedding preparations for their bright model daughter and her bright model fiancé. He had graduated with distinction from the Faculty of Law which was considered among the top faculties, along with the Police Academy and the Military College. It was enough to have a Law degree, or carry a star on your shoulder, to conquer the hearts of teenage girls.

But at nineteen, my friend, I was probably just like your

granddaughter. My heart wasn't going to be conquered by any man, let alone a member of the police or the military or law establishments. I wasn't just a teenager as they thought. I saw clearly that something was wrong with the world, with the entire universe, that everything was upside down and distorted. I understood that the noblest are trapped at the bottom of the pyramid: the lowest are at the top and the best are pushed low. Heaven was under my feet and not over my head. I walked through the dark night until I found the train to the other world. I paid the number of my years in pennies for a one-way ticket, and had four pence left in my pocket, not enough for a return ticket.

I was filled with happiness as I stepped towards a better world. I was overjoyed by the thought that I would never go back, even if it hurt to miss my mother and my little sister. I didn't have the price of a return ticket, and even if I did, I wouldn't go back.

Good-bye my friend in your faraway world, and don't worry about your granddaughter – I'm sure she's fine.

Nour's Buried Memories

My grandmother takes her place on the sofa in the spacious living room in the big house. The name of my grandfather the pasha is engraved in a shiny bronze plaque above the door and in the gold ring which has stayed around her finger since their marriage. The embossed letters scrape the skin of her finger every time she moves it. For instance, when she brought it to her face to lift the veil from her eyes, as the ship carried her over the Mediterranean waves, when she was only thirteen years old. Her face was hidden under a light white *bisha* embroidered with black dots and a thick blue burqa.

The pasha's new wife went to the French school, the Mère de Dieu, while I went to the English school. We played together during the summer holidays, when the family gathered at the big house on Queen Nazli Street.

The pasha was sixty-seven, short and slender with a puffy face. In the military barracks, he learned to blindly obey his superiors and tyrannise his subordinates – a historically established contradiction that students were taught during military as well as religious training, in Arabic and in English. As a marching soldier, he kicked his leg high in the air, pointing the tip of his shoe towards the gods in heaven, and once the war was over, he prostrated himself on the ground before the same gods, to thank them for victory or defeat, as long as he wasn't killed and didn't lose a limb. He rubbed his forehead in the dust in gratitude for having been granted a new life, then bathed himself with water and soap, dabbed some Eau Sauvage – the perfume that, in French, invokes savagery – under his armpits and between his thighs, put on his civilian clothes, and went to dance with those of his colleagues who had survived. He gambled and drank and fooled around with loose sensuous women, got his fill from worldly pleasures, then returned home at dawn and lay next to his wife, the pure mother.

She smelled his breath in her sleep and turned to the other side, her back turned to him, facing the wall. But the odour stayed in her nostrils. Even if she washed out her nose and used nasal drops and disinfectants, the rotten smell clung to the mucous membrane at the back of her throat.

She slept and dreamt that he had died and woke up beaming. In the shower she sang, 'Rejoice, my heart', until she heard him cough or blow his nose. When she found him in his chair on the balcony, reading the newspapers, she froze. A wave of depression washed over her.

His features were stone-like. The bridge of his nose was thick, and his lips were thin and taut like electric wires. He only ever smiled at the mirror. Standing before it to comb his moustache, he saluted himself: 'Pasha, your excellency.' The mirror smiled back, he laughed and greeted himself again, 'Welcome, Kamal Pasha.' He first put on a military costume for Eid when he was three years old. It was when his father started calling him Kamal Pasha. After the calves and the sheep were slaughtered, he went out with a toy gun and firework. The Turkish nanny bowed before him as he sat on his potty, calling him 'your excellency' before he'd even learned to use the toilet.

That man was my maternal grandfather. The first time he laid eyes on me, when I was breastfeeding in my mother's arms, he pursed his lips in contempt and spat out a grey slimy substance which the servants did not dare wipe off the Persian rug. Everything that came out of my grandfather's body was considered sacred, even his spit or snot, which he produced in copious amounts. He coughed a lot, a loud chesty cough mixed with cigarette smoke and the smell of booze, or ethanol as my grandmother referred to it.

My grandmother was light-skinned and so pale she almost looked bloodless. Her eyes were the colour of ashes, her irises always looking out from under water, forever trapped beneath a layer of frozen tears. But she saw clearly everything that went on in the house. Her domain was the back salon, filled with sofas and gold leaf chairs, marble tables and Persian rugs, silk curtains embroidered with green birds of paradise, purple pansy flowers and white jasmine. There were big windows overlooking the back garden. Female guests were received in this salon, while the men sat in the bigger salon that overlooked the front garden, its walls covered in wallpaper and the faces of sultans and kings looking out of gilded frames, sometimes on horseback, brandishing their weapons and medals:

King of England, Napoleon Bonaparte, Grand Sultan of Turkey, King of Egypt, and his son Farouk in the arms of his mother Queen Nazli, white and soft, half her face hidden behind a *yashmak*.

Through the open door of the back salon, my grandmother watches the women glimmering under the electric lights, their silk dresses revealing marble-smooth shoulders and white necks encircled by pearls and diamonds, diamond earrings dangling from their ears, their faces radiant and made-up, lips painted red, eyelashes fluttering and luxuriant. Their long locks, black or brown or golden blonde, sways in tandem with their soft laughter. In their midst sits her daughter, Zahiya Hanem, daughter of Kamal Hekmat Pasha, wife of Mohamed Sami Bey, carrying me on her lap.

My grandmother's eyes focus on her granddaughter. I can't walk yet, but I slip out of my soft and pale mother's arms and begin to crawl, black eyes alert, towards a specific goal. The stubborn persistence in my movements reminds my grandmother of herself when she was at that age, as she watches on with her clouded eyes. I crawl on the red, yellow and green Persian rug until I reach the polished wooden floor and keep on crawling. I reach the tiled corridor outside the salon, where the women have taken off their high-heeled shoes and left them with their light silk stockings on the floor. These visits last for hours and include lunch and dinner. It is hot in August when the family always gathers at the big house. My mother, Zahiya Hanem, has also kicked off her shoes and stockings and walks barefoot. Just as, every night, she throws off her nightdress and jumps into bed next to her husband, Sami Bey.

I watch my mother with attentive eyes. My bright black irises are now fixed on my mother's shoes and stockings, worried she might lose them in the chaos of the other footwear. My grandmother watches as I close my tiny fingers around my mother's shoes, the stockings carefully stuffed inside, and crawl back towards my mother who is deep in conversation, not paying attention to what is going on. But the grandmother does not take her eyes off her granddaughter. I am resolute in rescuing my mother's shoes and stockings. My mother sits in a *fauteuille* with a high gilded back and silver upholstery dotted with small colourful flowers, her soft hand resting on the gilded arm. I crawl until I reach her and deposit my prize in the safe fort underneath her massive chair.

In the quiet after the guests had left, my grandmother whispered to my mother, 'This daughter of yours, if she lives, will grow up to be a very clever girl.' My mother told me this story one year after my grandmother's death. I was nine years old and studying at the English primary school. Maryam was eleven, studying at the Mère de Dieu. She used to tease me saying that French was a finer language than English, and that her father's rank was higher than my father's. I hit her with the ball on her head and my mother scolded me, 'You shouldn't hit your Auntie Maryam.' My aunt Maryam stuck her tongue out at me and said, 'From now on you have to call me Auntie Maryam.' I stuck my tongue back out, 'I don't give a toss about your auntiness!'

Female babies died young. Boys were more valued and received better care, while little girls got nothing but negligence and veiled disgust. My mother was herself fifteen when I was born. She left me crawling on the floor and lost herself in fun and conversation with the guests, or left me in the care of the maid Salima and went out to the cinema or theatre. One night, Salima dozed off while sitting by the window and holding me to her chest, and I fell into the garden. It was a low-level window and the lawn outside was moist and soft, so I was fine. Still, Salima was severely punished. She was a child herself, just nine years old. My mother Zahiya Hanem and my father Sami Bey took turns beating her with the wooden broomstick until her nose bled.

That night I crawled to sleep next to Salima. I kissed her curly black hair. She cried as she held me. In the morning she received another beating. I understood little of what was going on around me. I loved Salima more than my mother and father. But one morning I woke up and didn't find her. An unfamiliar heavy feeling crept into my heart, which I later understood to be sadness.

'This girl is strange, Zahiya,' said my grandmother to her daughter at home. At school the teacher told the headmistress, 'This girl is headstrong, stubborn as a mule. She's not scared of getting beaten up or of burning in hell.' The teacher was called Zakariya Effendi. He was tall and stooped, had a hook nose and narrow deep-set eyes. He wet his finger with his saliva to turn the pages of the Qur'an. The girls and boys would be busy with their assigned tasks, bent over their copybooks reading and writing. They didn't see the teacher's saliva moistening God's holy name. But I was observant. I noticed too if the teacher scratched himself between his legs. He would eye me angrily. This child was different from the others. My eyes watched him shamelessly. I didn't look down when he looked at me like the other girls. The look in my eyes wasn't that of a child. I didn't stop staring at everything. Even when I looked in my book to read, my head remained unbent. I was nine years old and going to primary school. I liked school. I liked playing in the schoolyard with my friends, girls and boys. I liked running in open spaces and had dreams where I was flying like a bird in the air or swimming like a fish in the sea. I liked to dance and sing with the other girls at school.

A few years earlier, one day I found my father sitting in the balcony in his striped pyjamas, drinking coffee and reading the newspaper. He was summarising the news to my mother: A treaty was signed between Egypt and Britain, stipulating that British troupes should move to the Suez Canal area, limit their numbers to ten thousand soldiers and four hundred pilots, that British forces should remain in Alexandria for eight years, and that the Egyptian government is committed to offer help and resources to the British in the case of war.

My father was angry. 'The British will never keep their promise,' he said. 'This Anglo-Egyptian Treaty is a reaffirmation of colonialism not independence.' It was August 1936, and I was four and a half, staring at the letters in the newspaper as my father spoke. In 1950, al-Nahhas cabinet demanded new negotiations with Britain. Those negotiations went on for nine months and resulted in nothing but more colonial intransigence. Protests broke out demanding that Nahhas cut the negotiations short and cancel the treaty. Finally, it was unilaterally abrogated in 1951.

A Study of Philosophy and Change

(from Nawal El Saadawi's notes)

Philosophy is not a mental sport that is only practised inside the head and deals with abstract theories, away from the ever-changing cycles of life. It is not separate from quotidian socio-political life, whether public or private, and it is connected to other branches of knowledge, like medicine, physics, mathematics, psychology, history and religion.

Specialisation is often responsible for separating philosophy from the rest of life. Systems of education, since knowledge was turned into sin, have been designed to obscure knowledge rather than reveal it, to muddle the mind and promote blind obedience for the powers that be, whether at state or family level, in heaven or on earth.

I've found pleasure in thinking since I was a child. I used to think about questions that occupy most children's minds, for instance: 'Who created the stars in the sky?' The answer was always the same: 'God.' Then came the next natural question: 'Who created God?'

The concept of 'godhood' confounds children like it does philosophers. When it comes to delving into so-called taboos or subjects held sacred, the minds of children sometime dare to tread where philosophers' don't. Philosophers are aware of the risks of imprisonment or exile, should they challenge political or religious authorities. Children have to be indoctrinated into that awareness at home and at school.

The meaning of the word 'Allah' changed according to the views of the people around me. My peasant grandmother used to say in her simple dialect, 'God is just and known to be reasonable.' My uncle the Azhar scholar used to say that the human mind is not equipped to really know God or understand his wisdom in creating injustice and evil. But my childish mind never accepted injustice. Not since the first time I experienced it, when I saw my father favour my brother just because he was a boy. I was better in school and more intelligent, so why was I treated as an inferior?

I learned from the teacher at school that God, according to grammar rules, was masculine and not feminine, and that God's book, the Qur'an, addressed males only, and that a man has double a woman's share in inheritance. When I wrote my mother's name on my copybook alongside my father's, the teacher crossed it out and told me off, 'Your surname is only your father's name!' I felt that was unfair to my mother. It was her, after all, who cared for me more than my father did.

I saw injustice around me in the lives of poverty-stricken peasant women and men in my family and my sad village in the middle of the Nile's delta. I asked: 'Where does poverty come from?' And the answer came: 'God creates some people rich and others poor. Everyone's degree of wealth is determined by Allah.'

My childish mind never accepted that injustice that was attributed to God. I thought, like my grandma said, that God was just and known to be reasonable. My brain never stopped asking the childish question, which occurs instinctively to all children at some point: 'Why would God be unfair to the poor, and to women, including my mother and me and my sisters?'

Oneness

In childhood, people experience the natural oneness between body, mind, soul, the universe and other people around them. That was also the nature of early life in old pre-slavery human civilisations. Human societies, in their childhood, were not savage nor built on war and murder and rape as most historians have imagined. Old civilisations – in Egypt, Babylonia, Persia, India, China, among others – had philosophies that were based on such unity; the unity of all existence with all its living beings including humans. And human beings were not comprised of just mankind, but mankind and womankind. Gods too were female and male. The primary goddess was Mother Nature.

Then came the fascination with socio-political developments that led to the advent of an ethos of slavery, dividing the universe into heaven and earth, and humans into body and soul, and society into masters and slaves. Women were

joined to the ranks of slaves. All of this happened gradually. When the social order transformed from matriarchal
to patriarchal in Ancient Egypt, for instance, the mother
didn't immediately lose her position in religious and political life. That only happened after the patriarchal order
had stabilised, with one heavenly God becoming the male
father of the whole of humanity. Following that, Adam
became the single origin of humans, and Eve merely a
subsidiary being branching out from his 'crooked rib'. In
other words, it was as if the female was birthed from the
male and not the other way around. In Arabic, humanity is referred to as *banu Adam*, 'the sons of Adam', and
not the sons and daughters of Adam and Eve. In the Old
Testament, Eve merely features as the origin of sin and
evil and disobedience, because she reached with her hand
– and her mind – for the tree of knowledge. In the Qur'an,
Eve's name doesn't feature at all. She is only mentioned as
Adam's wife, and both of them – in the dual form – are
said to have eaten from the tree (without naming the tree).
But, it's Adam alone – in the singular form – who received
the word from God and was pardoned. He alone – in the
singular form – is also taught the names of all things.

With the establishment of a slavery order came changes
in philosophy, language, religion, politics, and ethics that
turned maleness into the accepted standard. A new order
based on gendered division of labour assigned physical,
bodily work to women (and slaves), considering them to
be bodies with no mind, while intellectual work (philosophy) became the domain of (upper-class) men. Except that

for a while in Ancient Egypt, Nut remained the goddess
of the sky, while her consort Geb was the god of the earth.
Daughters inherited the throne through their mothers,
and the old trinity consisted of the mother, the daughter,
the father. With the changes that society underwent, the
father moved gradually from his position as the god of
the earth to the one God up in heaven, while the mother
descended from her seat to become a symbol of land and
fertility. The trinity changed to: the father, the son, the
holy spirit – where the holy spirit supplanted the mother
who had lost her name, and became identifiable only by
her husband or male son.

The early natural matriarchal philosophy was built on
the holistic unity of life, on collaboration and justice and
mercy and love. With the emergence of the slavery order
came philosophies of power, and the power of a ruling
father God who derives authority from the sacredness of
his divinity and not from justice and mercy. The goddess
Nut resisted that ethos when in 4988 BCE, Old Egypt, she
told her daughter Isis: 'I do not advise my daughter who
will inherit my throne to draw her authority from divine
sanctity. I advise her instead to be wise, merciful, and just.'

The tenet of justice and mercy was still resisting the
rising tide of the tenet of power based on accumulation of
money and absolute male authority in governance and at
home. Another example of the tenet of justice and mercy
is the following maxim from Ptahhotep: 'Live in the house
of kindliness, and fill your heart with mercy before filling
your case with gold.' Isis was a symbol of wisdom and her

sister Maat a symbol of justice. Isis was the goddess of life and light (and also knowledge) and she was depicted with a sun ring above her head. But with the transition into the system of absolute patriarchal authority, her consort Osiris was accorded wisdom, and his son Horus inherited the throne which no longer passed from mother to daughter.

Rereading history in the light of new progresses made in archaeology unmasks these old narratives and thereby reveals the truth.

Philosophy in Ancient Egypt

The word 'philosophy' is derived from the Greek root 'philo + sophia' meaning love of wisdom. Hypatia is an example of a female thinker and philosopher who was killed in Alexandria, Egypt, in the name of religion.

The philosophy of slavery started in Ancient Egypt with the idea of one father from whom everything descended and his son as the heir. Osiris became the heavenly god who leads the battle between good and evil, followed by his son Horus who fought against Set, the god of chaos, who had killed Osiris. Ipuwer, author of the *Ipuwer Papyrus*, was perhaps the first sociologist in Ancient Egypt. He raged against the slavery mentality, looked for the heavenly god in vain and prophesised the coming of a saviour.

The souls of the dead are supposed to recite from the *Book of the Dead* on the day of resurrection. As proof of no wrongdoing and of having followed the commands of the pharaoh god, ruler in heaven and on earth, the dead recite: 'Glory be to you, great god of truth and justice. I have not sinned. I have done no evil. I have not reduced the measuring vessel or added to the pan of the scales. I am pure, pure.'

Akhenaten and Nefertiti were inspired by the *Book of the Dead*, developed in Thebes, but they only took from it the tenets on integrity in dealing with others. Perhaps because they worked under the guidance of Akhenaten's mother Tiye, they left out the tyrannical patriarchal parts. The two of them, together with Tiye, started a political, religious, ethical and social revolution in Egypt, in an attempt to re-establish the old values of justice and mercy and oneness and humanity. Akhenaten was depicted with a body more female than male, and as a just human god whose sky oversaw the earth with a maternal tenderness, and whose sun brought the light of truth and knowledge, which was the same image associated with Isis who carried the sun ring above her head and indiscriminately spread the light of wisdom and knowledge. The worship of multiple – male and female – deities never caused the sun to withhold its light. All humans were equal under the sun.

The hymns of Isis and Osiris, and of Akhenaten and Nefertiti (and Tiye), were directed at the goddess of wisdom, like the following hymn from the time of Isis:

O Isis, light-giver,
Grower of crops in the land,
Who brings forth life from her womb,

Like a hatchling from a bird's egg,
O mother of all life,
Life of the world,
Supreme mother of the universe.

With the transition to the patriarchal order, hymns like this changed. The labour of Tiye the mother and Nefertiti the wife was erased from history, and philosophy and knowledge and hymns were appropriated for Akhenaten alone.

Some believe Moses took certain Akhenaten hymns and made them the basis of his tenets for Judaism. In the Old Testament, the name of Eve shares the same root as the word for 'life', and her fall from grace ensures that the new paternal god has no competition in the form of maternal life. The concept of one heavenly god was taken from Akhenaton, who said, 'The Nile in heaven gives living water to strangers in all the lands.' And, 'Aten (sun god) lives in the hearts of humans.' It was also Akhenaten who ordered the destruction of the idols of previous gods and closed their temples, then abandoned wicked and unjust Thebes to build a new capital at Amarna dedicated to the worship of Aten. Isn't this what political change looks like whenever a new prophet or king or president comes along with new ideas?

But when conflict between the new king and the priests of past kings broke out and left Akhenaten and Nefertiti defeated, the new rulers destroyed their statues and left no trace of them.

Persian philosophy

Zoroaster inherited the conflict between body and soul, and between good and evil. Philosophy was separated from politics and disassociated itself from social movements that resisted the tenets of slavery. The king of kings in Persia was an unjust tyrant like the pharaoh in Egypt. His eyes and spies were everywhere, reporting back the sentiments hidden in the hearts of his subjects.

The king once killed a young man with an arrow then asked the victim's father what he thought. The slave father prostrated himself on the ground, rubbed his forehead in the dust between the king's feet and said, 'There's no wisdom beyond your wisdom and no shot more accurate than that of your blessed hand, divine King of Kings!' The king had intended to kill him too for bringing a dissident son into the world, but he pardoned him when he found him to be a true believer.

The crime of disbelieving or not accepting the wisdom of the god-king was punishable by death. This 'crime' has existed since the start of the age of slavery and still exists today in many parts of the world, East and West. It has been instrumental throughout history in separating philosophy from religion and freezing intellectual thought, old and contemporary, inside fixed repetitive moulds that renew and bolster whatever belief happens to prevail in a given society and the religion of the state as stipulated in the constitution. Even when the constitution stipulates nothing of the sort, and even where church and state have been separated, the charge of blasphemy or atheism or dissent against the accepted authority has continued to intimidate philosophers and scholars through the ages, all the way up to the present.

Maternal care and philosophy

Divine miracles that foretell the birth of a prophet or philosopher or spiritual leader abound. In Persia, for instance, there were stories predicting the appearance of Zoroaster before he was born: 'The God of light heard the complaints of his people and send them a prophet whose strength would be their salvation.'

There was also the myth about how Zoroaster's mind was embodied in his mother, a noblewoman who appeared to him in flashes of lightning. From her he received his calling in life: To bring light to the children of darkness.

Similar myths have recurred in the biographies of most prophets: The mother-figure is the one who guides her prophet son toward wisdom. Many prophets and philosophers had no fathers, or at least not ones we hear about. Their wisdom is received from the mother, and it is she who saves them from the tyranny of the ruling powers. Moses was saved from being murdered by the pharaoh by his mother, Jesus was protected by his mother, and Muhammad was protected by Khadija from the wrath of the Quraysh.

When Zoroaster was born, he came to the world laughing, driving away the spirits of evil who had surrounded his mother. The whole of nature rejoiced in light, the wind and the rivers and the trees chanted the uniting mantra. The newborn's mother fed him with courage and wisdom, mercy and love of justice.

And when the mother of Prophet Muhammad predicted she was pregnant, she knew she was carrying a prophet because she saw the light. There was light everywhere. She went home shaking and crying: 'Cover me! Cover me!' And later, it was Khadija who was there to support the prophet, calming him then telling him to get up and go spread God's message.

Evil spirits would have killed Zoroaster if it weren't for his mother's strength and protection. Jesus's enemies would have killed him if it weren't for his mother, Maryam. And Khadija, the mother figure who was twenty years Muhammad's senior, was a rich and well-connected noblewoman who protected him from those among the Quraysh who would have harmed him.

Without the care of women and mothers, most prophets and philosophers would have perished. Mothers played an important role in developing the values of justice and mercy in the hearts and minds of those prophets and philosophers who all, across the different religions, had a shared dream: For justice to prevail over tyranny, to unite humanity under conditions of freedom and love, and to bring an end to inequality. Their symbol for this human and universal oneness was the name of God, the supreme conscience. Unfortunately, it is injustice, war, and slavery that prevail to this day and take on a variety of forms.

When Zoroaster asked himself, 'What is God's purpose

behind the existence of evil, injustice, and war?', he started to doubt God's wisdom and justice, and even existence. His quest for God as oneness is represented in the texts that now make part of the Zoroastrian book, *Avesta*, where God is manifested in social justice, collaboration, equality, love and fraternity. 'If you know truth, you know God. God is justice,' says Zoroaster. Which is the same definition I heard from my peasant grandmother when I was six years old: 'God is just and known to be reasonable.'

Philosophers in Ancient Greece and in the modern West were influenced by the old philosophies of Egypt, Persia, India and China – just like the prophets before them. Old stories and mythologies journeyed with trade and travel, from philosophy books to religious teachings. Which is why a myth like that of Adam and Eve keeps recurring in different forms.

In Persia, for instance, the god Ahura Mazda created a woman and a man out of clay and gave them a blessed garden to live in, a paradise. The couple lived and worked together, loving and serving each other equally, following the old tenets of justice, collaboration, and love. But when they died, conflict broke out between their male and female offspring. The males turned to violence and fought over control and inheritance, forgetting the tenets of justice and collaboration. Ahura Mazda sent them a flood of melted ice (just like in the story of Noah's flood), and all drowned bar a minority of males and females who constituted an upgraded version of the species, more refined and more inclined towards justice and collaboration. Thus,

Ahura Mazda continued to experiment with the human clay in the hope of evolving the species towards a better, more just and collaborative version of themselves.

This story mirrors the ongoing journey of philosophers and scientists towards creating a better world. It also reflects the journey of matter, from the simplest organism – the amoeba – all the way to the highest form of life which is the merciful, just human for philosophers of materialism or idealism, and God for religious believers.

The battle between Ahura Mazda (the god of goodness and light) and Ahriman (the god of evil and darkness; or in other words, the devil) is a battle that started with the philosophy of enslavement. It is a futile battle, endless because it is unnatural, set as it is against the oneness of existence. Both darkness and light exist in the world – night cannot be disconnected from day, or body from mind, or matter from soul, which is a way to describe the invisible energy that matter emanates, like electricity or atomic power or other forms of energy.

Scientific discoveries have contributed to the development of philosophical ideas, just like free philosophical thought, when liberated from the prison of fear, has led to the development of more open scientific horizons.

Indian philosophy

We need to consider the unity of body and mind, of darkness and light, of good and evil, of matter and soul, to understand the following idea: Evil is the force generated by the goodness of God. The apparent contradiction of this statement reflects a religious idea that has evolved to form the basis of idealist and materialist philosophies and dialectics. It's an idea as old as the matriarchal civilisations of Egypt, Babylon and India, all premised on the oneness of the universe and the fusion of life and death in a never-ending cycle.

The Upanishads are ancient Sanskrit texts that bring together the philosophical ideas of women and men in India between the 7th and 5th centuries BCE. The core message of these texts is as follows: Pull yourself away from base desire, and if you fail and die failing, do not despair, for you will be born again and repeat the cycle. Death is not the end of life. Pain is as necessary to happiness as darkness is to light, and death is to life.

Gautama Buddha

Buddha put the Upanishads philosophy to practice in his life. Like the mothers of other prophets, his mother too had a dream about giving birth to a special child who would save the world. He is said to have been born clean, unstained by the blood and impurities of his mother's body. Let's stop for a moment here to contemplate this idea of masculine purity extracted out of feminine impurity, like a clean green plant from the unclean soil. This is another subjugating concept which divides the oneness of humanity into a defiled body (female) and an exalted soul (male), similar to how Eve's 'sin' always associates women with the evil of the devil, with impurity, filth, soil, a body without mind or with an inadequate mind.

This duality, or dichotomy, between masculinity and femininity still dominates religion and philosophy to this day. According to the Old Testament, a postpartum mother remains 'impure' for fourteen days if she has given birth to a girl, and for half that time if the newborn is a boy. All religious and philosophical texts abound with the notion of the superiority of masculinity over femininity, when it is in fact women who have preserved humanity from extinction, and who have protected prophets in their cradles.

The same applies to Buddha and his mother who rescued him from being killed by their enemies, only to be abandoned in the futile search for the pure god-father. He then got married and was given a son, only to abandon his wife and return to his quest. The devil tried to lure him back to his mother and wife and son, but he resisted. He wished to attain wisdom through pain and hunger, imagining that he could only reach the soul by passing through a perished body. But instead of finding transcendence, he encountered nothing but starvation. When he ate and satisfied his body once more, he thought again of the tediously repetitive cycle of life: birth, youth, old age, death, *ad infinitum*. Eventually he reached Nirvana, that is the state of enlightenment and selfless happiness that makes room for justice and mercy for all living beings including humans. He preached mercy and lovingkindness, and worshipped Brahma as the epitome of justice and goodness.

In the end, Buddha's ideas did not stray far from the wise words of my peasant grandmother: 'God is just and known to be reasonable.' He didn't consider himself a god-sent messenger, but rather a human explorer who discovered the natural laws of life that shall bring happiness to those who practise humanity, mercy, and kindness. Echoing St Paul's message to the Corinthians, he said, 'Like a caring mother, holding and guarding the life of her only child, so with a boundless heart of lovingkindness, hold yourself and all beings as your beloved children.'

And so, having matured, Buddha returns at the end of his journey to the ideals of the mother he had abandoned in his youth.

Chinese philosophy

In old China, philosophers were granted higher titles than military and political leaders. At the time of Confucius (around 400–500 BCE), old Chinese philosophy already included beliefs about evolution. The essence of wisdom was to give unconditionally, like Mother Nature. Happiness lay in collective success that achieves justice and freedom and love for all.

Lao-Tzu (who is supposed to have lived around 600 century BCE) was raised by his mother without a father. He learned about philosophy, music, and art, and understood that an independent mother is as good as a father, and as capable of providing for the household, and that she only loses her autonomy if she stays at home and forgoes paid labour. Lao-Tzu understood that the division of labour between mothers and fathers based on gender results in mothers losing their rights, in the family and wider society, and being written out of history (an idea that dominates contemporary feminism). He also saw that the justice of the state and the integrity of the individual start from the family, uncovered the links between the private and the public, between gender and economic oppression. To the rich he said that they must end their greed before the hungry stop stealing.

Because he fought the tenets of slavery that oppressed women and the poor, he was persecuted by the ruling emperor, threatened and pelted with stones by the emperor's followers. When the throne went to the next-in-line, Lao-Tzu was appointed Chief Justice, but was removed ultimately when he ruled justly – there are parallels here to draw with the life of Ibn Rushd (Averroes).

Confucian philosophy states that truth and justice are the essence of the law. When it speaks about superior persons, it's on the assumption that they are as refined as the justice and respect they achieve by working on others' behalf. This is different from Nietzsche's concept of a superman who is master over others. In this, Chinese philosophy did not diverge much from the Ancient Egyptian philosophy of Nut and Isis.

Greek philosophy heralding political and scientific progress

Philosophy in Ancient Greece moved away from con-templating the nature of godhood towards a scientific exploration of the make-up of the universe, from singular divine sanctity towards the sacredness of collective work (see again the ideals of Nut and Isis). There were materi-alists like Thales, Heraclitus, Socrates, Democritus, and Epicurus, who, regardless of their different approaches, converged on bringing philosophy down to earth and making it serve the enslaved majority and play a part in liberating them.

Thales is known for breaking from the use of mythol-ogy and instead using logical methods to explain the world. He believed that water held the originating prin-ciple of all matter.

Anaximander was Thales's student. He pioneered the idea of a primordial matter from which all forms of life and living being, including humans, originate.

Heraclitus considered fire as the most fundamental element in existence. He argued that fire is ever-changing because change is the fundamental law of nature. Heracli-tus famously said, 'You can't step in the same river twice.' He saw the world in terms of a tension between opposites that produces new, more evolved forms. In other words, there is oneness within perpetual change, or harmony within diversity and difference. Heraclitus's thought might have been the philosophical seed needed to trigger change from dictatorship and tyranny to tolerance and acceptance of difference, i.e. the basis of what we now call democracy.

Democritus's study of science and medicine helped him develop a philosophy based on deconstruction and analysis, followed by synthesis and construction, which is the unending rational process grounded in material realism. Democritus explored and studied the material world of the atom. He saw in every atom an internal living soul that determines its movement, thus edging closer towards the scientific discovery that proved that the second nucleus in the atom is composed of energy, not matter. Up to that point matter was considered to be based on the four elements: water, fire, air, earth. Democritus pioneered the idea of the atom being the principal element, and primordial matter consisting of an infinite number of indivisible atoms.

Today we know that the atom and nucleus can be divided, and finally even the electron. The particle smaller than the electron is called the quark, and even smaller particles can be measured with a unit called the 'nano'.

It has also been established that energy isn't an internal soul, but a form of matter, and that a quark moves at such incredible speed it can be detected in two places at once. All that transforms some of what used to be considered hard science. Philosophers today – men and women – continue to ponder these new scientific truths, hence fundamentally changing their understanding of the 'soul'.

Xenophanes returned in his philosophy to the idea of one world overseen by one infinite creator. He based his monotheism on the basis of the oneness of existence, and the premise that God exists in everything because he is everything. There are a lot of similarities here with Spinoza's pantheism which stipulates that God resides in everything, and nothing is like God because he is all things, all in one.

Pythagoras, on the other hand, saw God's invisible oneness embodied in the musical harmony of planetary movements. He was a mathematician who connected the principles of music and mathematics, and considered mathematics the highest form of philosophy. He built a commune of women and men who owned everything together and worked together. For him, private property was a source of misery and injustice in the world. He wanted to create something like communal socialism, what later came to be known as communism. His influence on later philosophers is palpable, from Socrates to Bertrand Russell and Karl Marx.

But it was **Socrates** who truly brought philosophy down from heaven and grounded it on earth. And he paid the price with his life. He was a materialist philosopher and a politician, and therein lay the danger. Class-based patriarchal orders in all their forms – be it feudal or capitalist, old or modern or postmodern – have always welcomed philosophers – materialist and idealist, religious and atheist – as long as they remain locked away in their ivory towers, far from people and politics and public life. That is, as long as they have no real impact or power to affect political change.

Aristotle and Plato gained respect and recognition from the state for one simple reason (which they share with the bulk of the intellectual elite across the East and the West, past and present) – they never stepped into people's reality. When Aristotle eventually did partake in political life, he too paid the price. As for Socrates, he was sentenced to death by drinking poison.

Socrates was only briefly involved in politics – he said that it was not a field for an honest person – but he was constantly preoccupied with the problem of oppression. He was strong of mind and body, and his strength was manifested in his tenderness and the merciful look in his eyes. He held that knowledge is the means to personal virtue and social justice.

He criticised the hypocrisy of the rulers and fake democracy that relies on the votes of the uninformed public. His criticism, uttered four and half centuries before the birth of Christ, too perfectly sums up our political affairs in the twenty-first century.

He was accused of blasphemy and of working to destabilise the state – the favoured charges against thinkers who are committed to justice and freedom. These are also charges that are designed to intimidate onlookers, so that they remain silent, give up any ideals they might have and join the chorus of hypocrisy.

Socrates was trialled before a jury of 500 members of the public who knew nothing about his thoughts but had heard rumours spread by the authorities suggesting that he was a reckless atheist clown who morally corrupted Athenian youth and was only interested in his own gains. In his defence, Socrates challenged his persecutors, 'You accuse me of working for my own gains and I've gained nothing but poverty. All I have worked for is justice. Are you not ashamed of acquiring riches and seeking no truth or understanding, or the perfection of your soul?' He vowed to never cease from 'rousing, persuading, and reproving' in order to expose contradictions and ignorance. When time came for his execution, the jailer cried as he brought the poison. Like everyone who got to know Socrates, he had come to love him.

Perhaps Socrates is the most humane philosopher for me, and the one I relate to most, because I have faced the same accusations in my own lifetime. I too have been imprisoned, except that the ruler who put me there was assassinated, while I made new friends in prison and left without drinking any poison.

Doesn't the same story recur wherever there is a human being who thinks for themselves? Especially in counties like ours, where the ruler is pharaoh-like, peerless and omnipotent.

Despite the greatness and timelessness that **Plato**'s ideas have attained, I've never liked them. Plato's utopian republic never appealed to me either, because it was just a cerebral utopia, divorced from reality. It contains only laws and deep insights, and offers a system where law, philosophy, state, religion, happiness, art and music are linked. But it's an earthly enough paradise that retains the existing classist, racist, patriarchal biases to make me renounce it. It's a beautiful, seemingly just, democratic republic that lacks true freedom and is devoid of love.

Aristotle, one of the greats in the history of philosophy, grew up close to Philip II of Macedon – they might
have played together as children – and later became the
tutor to his son, Alexander the Great. What happened to
his great nephew, Callisthenes, might have taught Aristotle caution in his dealings with kings. Callisthenes was
intelligent and rebellious enough to question Alexander's
divinity and refuse the practice of prostrating before him.
As a result, he was implicated in conspiracy and killed,
with no consideration to his uncle's feelings who was the
king's tutor.

Aristotle differs from Plato on a fundamental premise:
Plato considered that life is moved by external forces, while
Aristotle saw these forces to be internal. Both believed in
the existence of a divine force. Plato's God was idealist, a
creator of models, dynamic. Whereas Aristotle's God was
the unmoving mover, affecting the world while himself
remained unaffected. For him, God was a pure energy or
spirit that was never created but was a creator.

Aristotle opposed Plato's idealist utopia and found it
unrealistic. He rejected the idea of dividing wealth equally
among all people, saying that it would abolish individual
responsibility.

One day he found the courage to criticise Alexander,
but Alexander died suddenly before he could punish his
former teacher. After his death, Athens turned against
Macedonians and Aristotle, having been accused of
treason and blasphemy and fearing for his life, escaped
to the island of Euboea in the Aegean Sea. When he died,

he left behind a will freeing his slaves, perhaps finally going against his doctrine which stated that slavery is just and necessitated by the nature of slaves and women! His ideas in biology – claiming that the foetus is created by the male sperm alone, and that women are nothing but vessels – have been proven baseless, along with his theories in astronomy.

His views on the role of philosophy itself, however, were progressive, insisting that philosophy has to act like a guiding beacon for the socio-political order.

Diogenes was braver than Aristotle. He did not fear death. Why would he when he was the one who said, 'My life was lost the day I was born.' He also said, 'Aristotle dines when it seems good to King Philip, but Diogenes dines when he pleases.' He rejected private property in any form (as did Pythagoras) and called for abolishing slavery and establishing equality under a just law.

He said, 'The only pleasure lies in despising all pleasures.' He walked the streets to teach people like Socrates did. And he held that self-discipline is the only freedom, and that true security lies in rejecting wealth.

Epicurus pushed materialist philosophy forward. He grew up with an aversion to all forms of religious superstition. Like all children, he asked the question: 'Who created God?' Or, in his case, who created *hyle*, the primary matter? Finding no answers from teachers and philosophers, he began to search on his own. Having realised that God was the creator of good and evil, of pleasure and pain, he developed his doctrine that is based on pleasure and happiness. If humans only own the present moment, all they can do is live it as best as they can.

Epicurus held that the universe is made up of individual particles that move at high speed and swerve spontaneously outside of the existing *hyle* and back. These particles have different sizes and shapes that combine in endless permutations, and their movement creates the stars, planets, moons, suns and the rest of the infinite universe.

This idea was the seed that led to the development of modern cosmology. Epicurus also realised that our world is not the only one in existence, that there might be other worlds and other universes we're unaware of, and that this universe is gradually progressing towards its end, turning into cold dust.

Epicurus championed evolutionary ideas. He said that life and humans evolve through their struggle for survival. He maintained that death is nothing but a peaceful dreamless sleep, and that if our non-existence didn't bother us before we were born, why should it bother us after our death?

He also said that no reasonable god would command the building of a temple only to destroy it by lightning.

Monotheist philosophies

It could be said that the semi-monotheist philosophy of Nefertiti and Akhenaten paved the way for the prophets that followed: Abraham, Isaac, Ishmael, Jacob, Moses, Jesus, Muhammad. The three major monotheist religions, with their sects and branches, have played significant roles in revolutions and in bringing about socio-political, economic and ethical changes across the five continents. They established the patriarchal order on religious grounds and divine texts, which have become the main sources for constitutions and laws and ideologies in the East and West.

The three monotheistic religious texts – the Old Testament, the Bible, and the Qur'an – played a major part in making these changes happen, which in some cases meant fighting against slavery, on the premise that the only master is God.

Although some religious texts have retained a measure of approval for some forms of slavery, for instance when it comes to prisoners of war, and others outright permit owning slaves and concubines, all in all such fragments have been suspended and abolished by popular revolutions, resistance from slaves and women and the poor, and socio-economic changes. Thinkers and philosophers – men and women, from all over the world – have played a part in eradicating slavery and various aspects of the enslavement mentality.

However, ruling powers have always held on to texts and fixed ideas that safeguard their interests and put wealth and other people at their service. They have also always known how to buy philosophers and clergymen who would justify oppression and war on their behalf, all in the name of religion.

Words like 'God' or 'God's will' are often used as threats against those who work for justice and freedom, both of which are independent of race or gender or class. Such humane values have been promoted by male and female philosophers and prophets, starting from Isis and Osiris, Nefertiti and Akhenaton, all the way to Moses, Buddha, Confucius, Jesus and Muhammad, and from Socrates, Democritus, Aristotle and Epicurus, to Ibn Sina, Ibn Khaldun and Ibn Rushd, among many others.

But vicious conflict continues to this day, fueled by material profit, hiding under the cloaks of Judaism, Christianity, or Islam.

Prophets have faced death as often as other philosophers and thinkers, men and women, who fought against slavery and discrimination.

Many philosophers, however, failed to avoid the trap of dichotomies that is part of the tenets of enslavement, like the perceived contradictions between good and evil, human and god, black and white, master and slave, man and woman, body and mind, matter and soul. Here are some examples:

Like Christ before him, **Saint Augustine** was inspired by his mother who read to him from the Bible when he was a child. Then he forgot about his mother and the Bible and went through a phase of losing himself in the hedonism of youth. Until he wept one night and was addressed by a childlike voice that said: 'Get the book out and read! Read! Read!'

Augustine was a follower of Platonic thought and was influenced by the idealist philosophy that advocates discarding physical desires in order to be elevated towards

perfection, that is God. His view of women did not tran-
scend the perception of a sinning Eve who was the cause
of Adam's expulsion from paradise. He saw all women as
heirs to that sin, which made them inherently corrupt.

Thomas Aquinas held a similar view on women to
Augustine and some other saints. He considered her to be
the door to letting the devil in. He took the idea of God as
the ultimate cause of all things from Aristotle but disagreed
about the nature of God as unmoving, seeing him instead
as one who creates out of love. From the old philosophers
of Egypt and India, he took the concept of the humanity
of God and the divinity of humans. God for Aquinas lay
in the heart of every human being and was part of his/her
conscience. God was thus the collective conscience and
consciousness of humanity. He claimed that belief comes
before reason. But a hundred years earlier, came a Muslim
philosopher who asserted the opposite of that.

Ibn Rushd (known in the West as **Averroes**) held that
reason comes before belief, and that belief is built on
rational realisation according to the essence of Islamic
thought. Ibn Rushd was inspired by the dissident materialist rational trends within Islam, from Abu Dhar al-Ghi-
fari to the Khawarij and Mu'tazila, and the mystic Rabia
Basri who believed, like my peasant grandmother, in the
God of justice and love and mercy – not the God of heaven
and hell and holy texts.

Ibn Rushd, like any other thinker anywhere in the
world, was influenced by the scientific, political, and economic developments of his time. His rational philosophy

influenced and foretold the modern renaissance that came after him. But unjust governance, tyrannical rulers and foreign colonisers, led to the weakening of philosophers and the distortion of their ideas, to the degree that they were accused of apostasy and either banished or, at the very least, neglected and allowed to fade from remembered history.

That is why Ibn Rushd's ideas didn't spread to our part of the world. In spite of the fact that he was a practising Muslim and a believer, his ideas benefited later philosophers in Europe more than anyone in the Muslim world.

Ibn Rushd was born in Córdoba in 1126 CE and died in 1198 CE in Marrakesh: Decades of contemplating and fighting to preserve the core of philosophy and religion, that is justice. He was a critic of the idealist Neoplatonic tendencies of earlier Muslim philosophers like Ibn Sina and al-Farabi, and considered them steeped in fantasy and mysticism. He was a proponent of Aristotelian theories, engaged with them for a long time and tried to introduce them to his Muslim countrymen. In addition to philosophy, he also studied the science of *kalam* (discourse), theology, poetry, medicine, mathematics, and astronomy.

In 1182, when he was fifty-six years old, Ibn Rushd was appointed by the caliph Abu Yaqub Yusuf as court physician and judge in Córdoba, and remained in that position for ten years. He also served as a judge in Seville, and as court physician in Marrakesh. Yusuf commissioned many of Ibn Rushd's Aristotelian commentaries, but in 1195 – whether because his interpretations favoured rational thought over textual tradition, or at the instigation of other theologians whom the caliph needed to appease for political reasons – Ibn Rushd fell out of favour and was banished to Lucena. His books were burned, and he was banned from practising philosophy. He was eventually reinstated in Marrakesh, but died before receiving the caliph's pardon. Isn't he just another example of an honest philosopher who is not intimidated by the ruling powers into renouncing his ideas?

Modern philosophy and scientific progress

Astronomy replaced astrology, chemistry replaced alchemy, anthropology replaced stories about demons and spirits, Columbus discovered a new world beyond the sea, Copernicus discovered a new way to observe the stars, Galileo discovered that the earth is moving. And while the earth circled in space, ideas circulated inside various thinkers' heads. Philosophers began to dismiss the religious and philosophical superstitions of the dark ages, when nooses and beheadings were the fate threatening any disbeliever questioning God's – i.e. the king's – orders.

The victims were always more women than men, those daughters of Eve the sinner, wicked witches who dared question the teachings of the church and treat patients in newly invented ways. Which means that they offered alternatives to the holy water the priests monopolised and sold, directly from God who is the sole healer, not those infidel traitor medics and witches.

At school children used to chant 'God, Country, King' – in one breath, considering all three were one and the same. The political and religious powers were closely linked, and corruption was as ripe as ever.

Francis Bacon was knighted and appointed Attorney General by King James. His position, and fear of losing favour, meant that he colluded with the king and was implicated in corruption and advancing arbitrary policies. He had enemies in the parliament, and when circumstances eventually changed, they made sure that his career ended in disgrace. Once Bacon had lost the trinity of God, King and Country, he isolated himself and began to think about the state of a tumultuous world. He criticised his own past contradictions, which were based on greed and fear. For a period of time, Bacon had tried to confuse people with a stance that can be summed up in the phrase: 'Don't look to actions, but look to my books' (which was also a sentiment repeated by Naguib Mahfouz in Egypt). But separating action and thought is just like separating body and soul: A harmful philosophical dichotomy that allows all kinds of corruption, enslavement mentality, and injustice to filter through.

Bacon started to denounce this dichotomy. He asserted that unjust distribution of wealth is a primary reason for revolution and war, and also that knowledge means more than fortune and power. He rejected the vagueness of some of Aristotle's statements, such as God being the unmoving mover, or the uncreated creator. He said that philosophy should begin by using clear, accurate words, and that it should build on empirical experimentation like other branches of science. He held humans to be masters of the universe, and the highest intelligence to be that of God in heaven.

René Descartes started by doubting God's existence and concluded with confirming his existence. He started from a place of rational thinking, and that led him to a place of belief. He agreed with the scientists about the rotation of the earth, and was accused of atheism. But he persisted in his rational methods: 'I think, therefore I am.' Though he remained trapped within the inherited dualities that separate matter and soul, body and mind, woman and man, ruler and ruled. His trinity consisted of: 1) a physical body; 2) a thinking spirit; and 3) God who is in everything.

Baruch Spinoza saw the world as oneness (body and soul being a complete unit). His philosophy is known as pantheism (meaning that God resides in everything): God is in all, and all is one. He was banished and excommunicated from the Jewish congregation. They issued a *cherem* against him in which many curses were brought down on him, including the one uttered by Elisha – 'the Lord will rage against this man and bring upon him all the curses which are written in this book, and the Lord will blot out his name from under heaven' – but Spinoza's name has not been blotted out. It lives on and takes up more space in history than Elisha's.

Spinoza maintained that religions divide people and he wished to unite them. His persecution by those in power drove him to isolate himself in his room and watch the spiders, commenting on their similarities to humans when it comes to chasing flies!

He died at the age of 44 from a lung disease, his book *Political Treatise* still unfinished. He had hoped to change the world through politics, having failed to change it with philosophy. He made the same mistake made by most patriarchal philosophers, however, when he failed to break away from the idea that war was just a partial and incidental aspect of the wider and eternal universe.

Spinoza repeated the ideas that preceded him: That humans were like small worms in relation to the sacred whole, and that the human mind is unprepared for understanding the universe that is predetermined by forces beyond human will – a perception which leads to passivity in the face of unjust rulers. Still, Spinoza contributed to developing the concept of 'equal opportunity', and embraced the idea of a social collective, which lies at the heart of democracy. He advanced the ideals of justice and free humans being their own masters. He was attacked and ridiculed in his country because of his alleged atheism.

John Locke inspired the English and perhaps also the American revolutions (1688 and 1776). He made a leap from the idea of the absolutist rule of a monarch to the idea of democratic republican rule by the people. Locke studied medicine, philosophy, politics and various forms of governance. He differed from Bacon insofar as he didn't separate politics from everyday moral values – like honesty, integrity, justice, equality. He played an important role in promoting political intellectual freedom, rewriting laws and constitutions in favour of justice and equality. Naturally, he was persecuted in England and escaped to France, was persecuted there too and moved to Holland to live there in isolation from the politics of his country.

Locke left behind a philosophy based on clear thinking and concise language. He believed that true concepts can be expressed in a clear language. He was a proponent of multiplicity, tolerance, logical argumentation, and judgement following from reason. He didn't reject private property, and believed that it can be accumulated through hard work, as long as others have enough, in terms of quality and quantity (which is essentially a form of socialism). He remained a believer in the tenet of sacred justice (represented by God) which can be instinctively grasped. Government for Locke is based on a mutual contract based on independence, freedom and equality, with the power lying with the people not the king. He laid down the basis for the separation of powers into legislative, executive, and judiciary – with the highest authority given to the legislative power.

This philosophy was the seed that grew into American independence a hundred years after Locke's death. It inspired other thinkers from Jean-Jacques Rousseau and Voltaire in France to Gandhi in India.

When I turned sixteen in 1947, I was in love with reading philosophy and literature. I had discovered **Mahatma Gandhi**, the idealist Indian philosopher who fought his enemies not with violence but with love and passive resistance. But although his approach helped bring India its independence, it didn't save him from being assassinated at the hands of a member of an extremist group who was working to divide Hindus and Muslims and ultimately India itself to serve the interests of external and internal powers that were ready to pounce on her newly won independence.

The word 'passive' didn't appeal to me. It's a trait usually attached to women. Chivalry and bravery and dynamism were the traits of true manhood. While femininity was meant to be the opposite of all that: passivity and hesitation and weakness and cowardice. I was naturally rebellious since childhood against all those characteristics that were forcibly imposed on us as 'feminine'. I wasn't at all passive. I was braver and more active than my older brother!

I was moved by **Taha Hussein** and his writings. Despite being visually impaired – having lost his sight in early childhood – he was confident and proud of his intellect and insight. I loved his book *Al-Ayyam* (The Days) and could relate to it, even if the details and circumstances were completely different from my own experiences. He was a middle-aged renowned intellectual and I was a sixteen-year-old schoolgirl.

Taha Hussein's books were not part of the curriculum in secondary school. I remember that Abbas al-Aqqad's book about the life of the second caliph in Islam, *Abqari-yat 'Umar* (The Genius of Omar) was in the curriculum of my third year at Helwan Girls School, like it was in most schools around Egypt. But the books I liked to read, those that inspired me with new ideas, weren't in the curriculum and weren't easy to find.

I went on to study medicine despite my love of literature, philosophy and music. During my undergraduate years, my thinking faculties came to a halt – it's what happens to most students in our part of the world.

Taha Hussein wasn't considered a philosopher, but in my own honest opinion, he was a better philosopher than many who carried the title. Zaki Naguib Mahmoud, for instance, maintained that the philosopher is a neutral thinker who must remain uninvolved in political life. But that was only his excuse not to challenge the tyrannical ruling regime.